Slim & Fit Kids

Slim & Fit Kids

Raising Healthy Children in a Fast-Food World

Judy Mazel
author of the #1 bestseller *The Beverly Hills Diet*

John E. Monaco, M.D.

with Sheila Sobell

Health Communications, Inc.
Deerfield Beach, Florida

www.hci-online.com

The *Slim & Fit Kids* program is not intended as a substitute for the advice and/or medical care provided by your pediatrician or family physician, nor is it meant to discourage or dissuade you or your family from the advice of a physician. Your pediatrician or family physician should be regularly consulted in matters relating to your family's health, and especially with regard to symptoms that may require diagnosis. Any eating or lifestyle regimen should be undertaken under the direct supervision of a physician. Moreover, any individual with chronic or serious ailments should never undertake changes in his/her eating or lifestyle regimen unless under the direct supervision of their physician. If the reader has questions concerning the information presented in this book, or its application to his or her family's particular medical profile, or if the reader's family has unusual medical or nutritional needs or constraints that may conflict with the advice in this book, he or she should consult with their pediatrician or family physician. Individuals participating in this program should not stop prescription medications or any other treatment modalities without the advice or guidance of his or her personal physician.

Library of Congress Cataloging-in-Publication Data

Mazel, Judy.
    Slim & fit kids: raising healthy children in a fast-food world / Judy Mazel, John Monaco, with Sheila Sobell.
       p.   cm.
    Includes bibliographical references and index.
    ISBN 1-55874-729-X (trade paper)
    1. Obesity in children—Prevention.   2. Reducing diets.   3. Food combining.   4. Children—Health and hygiene.   I. Monaco, John. II. Sobell, Sheila.   III. Title.   IV. Title: Slim and fit kids.
RJ399.C6M396   1999
613'.0432—dc21   99-44490
                                                  CIP

Publisher: Health Communications, Inc.
              3201 S.W. 15th Street
              Deerfield Beach, FL 33442-8190

Cover design by Andrea Perrine Brower
Inside book design by Lawna Patterson Oldfield

Dedicated to
Paramahansa Yogananda

Other Books by Judy Mazel

The Beverly Hills Diet

The Beverly Hills Diet Lifetime Plan

The Beverly Hills Style

The New Beverly Hills Diet

The New Beverly Hills Diet Recipes to Forever

The New Beverly Hills Diet Little Skinny Companion

Contents

Part I. Childhood Obesity: Our Growing Problem

Part II. The Slim & Fit Program

Section I: Eating Slim & Fit

Section II: Thinking Slim & Fit

Section III: Moving Slim & Fit

Section IV: Slim & Fit Forever

Acknowledgments

Thank you John Monaco for being a "letter writer" as well as a Born-Again Skinny with a new passion; Sandee Kunz, Wheels McKee and Tara Rogachefsky for keeping the curtain up and the show going on . . . you made this possible; Sheila Sobell for coming onto the scene and showering us with your brilliance; Matthew Diener for vision, foresight and a third dimension; Bikram Choudhury for strength, stamina, endurance and flexibility; Pacific Athletic Club for your wealth of talent; Jessica Piha for making the connection; and my whole wonderful, incredible panel of experts and contributors who made this A BOOK: Thea White Riches, Mariane Karou, Christina Tsitrian, Francisco Cornejo Mena, Michael Szymanski, Ellen Jones, Carol Yellin, Janice Vander Pol, Barbara Bassill, Yvonne and Wayne Woods, Tara Rogachefsky and Lily Brumwell. Sarah Briane Cluster for keeping the energy flowing; Treasure Mazel for going with the flow . . . my special blessing; Pusha Cariolagian for being such a good listener and friend as well as the world's best manicurist; Ezra Woods for being such a good example; Gayle King and Jenelle Fiorito for bringing John Monaco into my life; Maraea Johnston for turning me toward the polestar when the ship was lost at sea; Margie and Herman Platt for being the best friends a girl could have; Yvonne and Wayne for coming out of the Woods and into my heart with lotus, love and a family; Joseph Woods for being skinny; Yvette McDaniels, Kelly Peterson and Dee Detruglia for copies faster than a speeding bullet and service above and beyond; Nancy Duncan for a grand opening and turning a deaf ear; Sr. Mukti Mata for faith and understanding; Paula Bambic for direction and support; Charles Werner, Nancy McBride, Lynn Acken, Susan Van de Bittner, Cynthia Watson and Gloria Kaye . . . especially Gloria Kaye for focus, alternatives, hope and TLC; Dana Scott and Erin Pollack for stepping in, taking over, and making it work better than ever—my pot Acre of gold at the end of the Rainbow; Brother Devananda for getting me to the right place at the right time, Brothers Bimalananda, Satyananda, Keshavanada and Brahamachari Simon for insight and inspiration; God and Gurus for guidance; and Paramahansa Yogananda for EVERYTHING.

God bless you all

Judy Mazel

My deepest gratitude and eternal admiration go to Judy Mazel for the vision, genius and sheer guts to include me in the creation of this book. She will forever be my comrade and my hero. Without the courage and intuition of Peter Vegso, the perseverance and understanding of Matthew Diener, and the enthusiasm of Kim Weiss and her team, this work would not have been possible. And thanks to Sheila Sobell for helping us to bring it home.

Immense thanks to Drs. Hamid Latif and Hector Pabon, without whose flexibility and understanding I would not have been able to spend endless hours researching, writing and rewriting. And to the medical staff and administration at Brandon Regional Hospital, I remain forever grateful. But to the Pediatric and PICU nurses at Brandon and Audubon Hospitals I shall remain always in your service. You are the true heroes of American healthcare.

I want to thank Mildred Rowell for passing on to me her kindness, compassion and optimism; Bob Bowman for making community critical care possible for me; Gewan Maharaj and Dan Johnson who give me optimism and hope; the University of Florida departments of Pediatrics and Critical Care for believing in me; Dr. Carmen Caltigerone and the fifth and sixth graders at the Academy of the Holy Names in Tampa; the American Academy of Pediatrics for their unwavering support of all aspects of children's lives and John and Marilyn for the lessons of a life well lived.

Janice, you would have loved this project, and believe me you were there every inch of the way. To Pam, Alex and John, without whom my life would be a veritable shell, I will love you always.

John Monaco, M.D.

Introduction

Dateline, U.S.A.

November 17, 1998—Syndicated in newspapers every-where, the lead story on television news shows across the country:

> *Childhood obesity is at epidemic levels in the United States. The U.S. Surgeon General, David Satcher, told the* Washington Post, *"Today we see a nation of young people seriously at risk, starting out obese and dooming them-selves to the difficult task of overcoming a tough illness."*

Look around you . . . you can't avoid seeing it. The sta-tistics are staggering, double what they were twenty years ago. One-third of our children are overweight, one in five obese.[1]

This frightens Dr. John Monaco because he sees kids all day, every day—he's a pediatrician—not the kind of pedia-trician you take your kids to for their regular exams or when they have a tummy ache or the flu. He doesn't see children on a regular basis in an office, but rather when the end is near, when they could be close to death, when one of their systems has failed, when they've been in a serious accident or attempted suicide. He's a pediatric critical-care physician, who heads the ICU (Intensive Care Unit) at Brandon Regional Hospital in Tampa, Florida. What has him so alarmed is that most of the kids he sees are fat and getting fatter and because of it, asthma is on the rise, as is the mortality rate. Type 2 adult diabetes is becoming prevalent in children, a first-time phenomenon. And, unlike type 1 diabetes, which is often congenital, type 2 is *self-induced,* the result of excess weight.

A high percentage of children diagnosed with attention deficit disorder (ADD) and hyperactivity are on drugs to balance out the chemical imbalances in their brains. But the problem may not be a chemical imbalance . . . perhaps it is the result of too many fitful, sleep-interrupted nights caused by sleep apnea, a condition in which breathing is obstructed by fat accumulations in the upper airway and diaphragm. A serious rise in bone and joint injuries are creating lifelong orthopedic disabilities because those little growing bones are too small to carry the excess weight imposed on them.

More and more young people today who attempt suicide are overweight. And what other correlation can you draw between the rise in teenage pregnancies than to the premature, increased sexual activity among young people due to early puberty? The culprit—the cause of early puberty—increased body fat!

Chubby used to be cute. But it's gone beyond baby fat, and it's not a pretty picture! The prognosis is grim, and if you are one of the millions of American parents with an overweight child, you're scared, too.

Your two-year-old is too heavy for you to pick up, let

alone carry. Your six-year-old doesn't want to go back to school because the other kids are making fun of him. Your eleven-year-old can fit in your clothes, and your nine-year-old has a bosom and pubic hair. Something is wrong here. Eight-pound babies aren't supposed to gain four pounds in two months. It's not natural . . . it's *not* a good thing. Nine-year-old girls aren't supposed to be menstruating. Were you? *Bigger* isn't better. We don't want our children in the upper percentile on the growth charts . . . this isn't the SATs!

Clothing manufacturers can't keep up with the growing market. They used to size baby clothes, by age; now that isn't even within the realm of possibility. Not when newborns are practically outgrowing their layette sets before they even leave the hospital, or they're wearing toddler-size three at six months. Even the disposable diaper manufacturers have jumped on the bandwagon; their extra, extra-large diapers are the first to need replacing on the supermarket shelves.

Whoever heard of eleven-pound babies, now commonplace, or seven-pound chickens? Is there a correlation? We'll get into that a bit later.

Why are kids getting so much bigger so much sooner? Evolution you say. . . . In one generation? Hereditary . . . the only thing about fat that is hereditary, and that can be "scientifically" proven, is eating habits. Fat kids eat the same food and the same way as their fat parents. Glandular . . . one in one thousand perhaps!

You have a right to be scared because if you've listened to the "experts" and their solutions—they don't have any.

The syndicated *Washington Post* article previously quoted continues, "Sedentary activities such as watching television and computer games are partly to blame. So is long-maligned junk food."

Not even Dr. William Dietz, the foremost authority in pediatric nutrition, has much more to offer. In the official complete home reference, *Guide to Your Child's Nutrition,* published by the American Academy of Pediatrics, co-authored with the equally prominent pediatrician Lorraine Stein and extensively reviewed by an advisory panel of experts, he recommends . . . *avoiding temptation, not limiting calories, but restricting them . . .* whatever that means . . . *increasing activity, reducing fats and drinking a minimum of twenty-four ounces, that is, three eight-ounce glasses of milk a day.* (Not only is *this* not the answer, *nothing,* you will soon learn, could be worse!)

Dr. Dietz also claims that if you, as a parent, are not overweight, your chubby toddler will slim down by age three.

Well, you aren't overweight and your once-chubby little toddler is now seven and looks like he is ready to be a line-backer for the Chicago Bears.

You're at your wits end. You've tried healthy snacks. You're cooking and eating more meals at home, as inconvenient as it is and as much as the rest of the family hates it, you're following the "Pyramid Plan" and spending your entire afternoon taking the kids from one physical activity to another. Soccer, gymnastics, swim class, dance—and it's not working. Your infant isn't weaned yet, and he's growing out of control. You don't understand it. Your pediatrician throws up his arms, shakes his head and rolls his eyes. He, too, like 80 million other Americans, is also overweight.

During this latter half of the twentieth century, the surgeon general has warned us of many dangers. Infectious diseases, environmental threats, drug abuse, deadly weapons, poverty and malnutrition . . . issues that threaten our lives as American citizens and our health as a people. On November 17, 1998, the surgeon general warned us of our latest threat. Now considered an epidemic, it is claiming as victims our most valuable natural resource, our children. It kills, it causes disease, distress and depression. It threatens the quality of life which our prosperous society has thus far provided. Now affecting at least one-third of our nation's young people, childhood obesity knows no sexual, cultural or socioeconomic barriers and affects every aspect of their lives. It is potentially more dangerous than all other public health issues combined, and yet by many opinion makers— the media included—this insidious threat is thought to be nothing more than a social inconvenience, a matter of cosmetics with a simple resolution.

The Tampa Tribune editorial that published the syndicated *Washington Post* article about childhood obesity went on to say "but overweight people, young or old, would do well to put the blame, not on hamburgers and pizza, but on themselves. Overweight people get that way and stay that way because they eat too much. Individuals who eat sparingly can eat almost anything and not get fat. Still, an apple is far more healthy than a bag of fries and it's up to the parents to set an example—and lay down the law."

Sloughed off, ignored and giggled about for too long, this killer, childhood obesity, has become the surgeon general's number-one priority for the twenty-first century. Now, it is up to us, and "the experts," to recognize it as the danger it is and fight it with every resource available.

Dr. John Monaco has taken up the gauntlet, entered into the fray and is prepared to win the battle. He has the solution!

Welcome to the world of *Slim & Fit Kids*, a world that will allow you to keep that wonderful ritual of eating a wonderful ritual. A world of eating and feeding your family that is fun, and conveniently easy, as well as nourishing, slimming and energizing. A way to ensure healthy, vibrant children once and for all . . . and forever. A way of ending the "Fat Crisis."

Join Dr. John Monaco and his coauthor, diet expert Judy Mazel, author of *The Beverly Hills Diet,* on this journey to slimhood and optimum health by learning a new way of nonrestrictive eating that doesn't include counting calories or fat grams, limiting portions or restricting fast food. This is a way of eating that, unlike our current practice, works with the digestive system, not against it—a way of eating that recognizes, acknowledges and utilizes all the current "state of the art" scientific data now available about the workings of our digestive systems, data that simply wasn't known to the scientific community when "eating" became an organized activity.

You see, being slim and fit has nothing to do with what you eat *or* how much you eat, but what you eat together. It's all in the combinations and the consciousness.

Combinations you will easily learn and adapt to, as well as a consciousness you will instill in yourself and in your child.

At long last, your problems are over. You are about to experience a revelation. You will be presented with scientifically documented information that is going to turn your life around, information that will dramatically alter your relationship to food, the way you feed your family, what you put in your shopping cart and how you feed yourself when you are pregnant to ensure that your unborn baby is not born with a "fat potential."

As you begin to understand food and eating from this new vantage point, you will reap *a plethora* of fringe benefits. Your "Chubby" will slim down; your entire family will look, feel and "behave" better; you'll reduce your grocery bill *by a lot;* and, you'll spend much less time running to the doctor.

But this book isn't just about how and what *foods* to "feed" kids, how to shop and how to create recipes. This program is much, much more. In the chapters that follow, you'll learn exactly how your body digests food, along with the simple steps you can take to maximize the natural efficiency of the digestive process—the key to weight control.

"Slim & Fit Kids" don't just eat right; equally important, they think right, too, particularly about themselves. How do you *redevelop* their self-esteem and sense of self, which has been so shattered by the burden of all those extra pounds? How do you rescue a sense of pride and inner security that has been buried and lain dormant under a fleshy cover? The tools will soon be yours.

Dr. Monaco and Judy Mazel grew up fat—fat at a time when they were in the minority. They've been there, done that and have come out as winners, as will your children. Together with the expertise of other professionals, they have created the "Slim & Fit Self-Esteem Program"; a collection of games . . . nonphysical exercises that will banish the negativity that has so plagued your child's young, vibrant life.

No, fat kids are not happy kids. On that, all the experts agree. The psychological and social consequences of growing up fat can and will continue into adulthood unless nipped in the bud and plucked from the vine. This is the essence of the "Slim & Fit Self-Esteem Program."

Slim & Fit eating means lots of energy. And to ensure that your kids are making the most of this newfound energy, Thea White Riches, a foremost authority on children's fitness and the director of the Children's Program at the illustrious Pacific Athletic Club in Pacific Palisades, California, has developed a series of ever-changing, fifteen-minute programs to keep those little feet moving and grooving . . . and having fun!

Then of course, there are the kids themselves, kids like Ezra Woods, who used to be fat, aren't fat anymore, and will never be fat again. "Out of the mouths of babes" emerge their success stories, their trials, their tribulations and their ultimate triumphs. So, sit back, relax and read on. Your problems are over, and your "little chubby" is now on his or her way to becoming a slim, healthy adult.

PART I

Childhood Obesity: Our Growing Problem

One

Obesity: My Personal Battleground

The Problem Hits Me in the Hospital

My pager beeps at 4:00 A.M., and I'm off to the emergency room to care for a four-year-old boy in the throes of an asthma attack. He weighs one hundred pounds. He requires immediate intervention.

I'm summoned to an outlying hospital at midnight where a fourteen-year-old diabetic girl is in shock and coma. She weighs 186 pounds.

An eight-year-old girl had always been overweight. For the last six months she had complained of knee and hip pain and her gym teacher noticed her limping. An orthopedic surgeon diagnosed a weight-related hip problem that requires immediate surgery.

Welcome to my world, where situations like this have become commonplace. I am a pediatric critical-care physician. This means that I spend my days, and often nights, in

3

a pediatric intensive care unit. Here I take care of children who are severely ill, whose simple cold has advanced to pneumonia, or whose diarrhea has advanced to dehydration and sometimes shock. In the course of dealing with these problems each day, I see more and more children whose weight is out of control and out of sight. If the fat kids I see are not physically ill because of their obesity, then they are in emotional pain because of it. In many cases, both are true.

The epidemic of childhood obesity is not a recent revelation to me. This problem has frustrated me for years. I have tried to talk to parents, but many are in denial, afraid people will think it's their "fault" that their kids are overweight. So they simply accept it or try to rationalize the problem away. . . . "I was a fat kid, too" or "Our whole family is big" are statements I often hear from parents who have decided to accept a situation they feel powerless over. . . . sometimes without even trying to fight it.

My colleagues in general pediatrics feel equally helpless in dealing with childhood obesity. "Kids are just getting fatter," they say. They blame junk food and TV and lack of physical education in schools. It is a complicated problem that they have not been trained to solve. In resignation, many say that it is only a cosmetic problem, whose medical effects will only be felt in adulthood.

Anyone who feels this way is missing the point. Any doctor, or parent, who refers to childhood obesity as simply a "cosmetic" problem needs to walk in my shoes for a few days. If they saw the situation from my perspective, they would see that fat can truly be life threatening. Day after day I see grossly overweight, asthmatic kids struggling to breathe . . . newly diagnosed diabetics, some with the *adult* form of the disease. I see young boys and girls so shy and lacking in self-esteem that after years of obesity they've shut themselves off from the joys of life.

Then there are the other children. Children whose lives may not be threatened, but their health and sense of self-worth are in peril because of their weight. Girls with bulging middles and wide backsides. Boys with double chins and breast development. When other children—and even parents and teachers—joke about their size, the kids themselves sometimes laugh along with them, in self-defense. But I know this is not sincere laughter. I know that inside their hearts are breaking.

They don't want to be fat, and they don't know why they *are* fat. They just know that one day they looked at themselves in the mirror and realized they were not like the other kids. They wonder why little Erica has a flat belly and slim legs, while they are all jiggly. They wonder what they could have done better, or what they did wrong. They want help, but no one seems to care. Well, I want you to know that I care, and now I have a solution, and with your help we are going to solve this problem and give these children their lives back!

Why do I care? Primarily, it's because children are my life and treating their pain and misery is my profession. But equally important . . . I've been there. I was a fat kid, too.

The Fat Kid: Facing Up to My Past

Fat oaf. That's what my family called me. Some still do. It was my identity. Like the overweight kids I work with, being fat was who I was. My weight dictated everything I did, or wasn't successful at doing. I was a scholastic "nerd" because I couldn't play athletics, date girls, wear cool clothes or hang out with the popular kids. Unless you've been there, you will never understand. Even now that I am no longer physically fat, I still think of myself as fat.

Even my mother still doesn't miss an opportunity to recount my transformation from a kid who was skinny as a rail until age nine—when my tonsils were taken out—to a fatty, forever relegated to shopping in the "husky" section for clothes. She doesn't mean anything by recounting these stories. To her they are endearing. But then, she was never a fat kid.

As far as the physical effects of being an overweight kid, I required knee surgery when I was fourteen, supposedly as the result of a football injury. Given how much I sat on the bench, this "injury" probably had more to do with my fatness than with my prowess as an athlete. My elevated blood pressure was first detected when I tried to donate blood in high school. The very first time my cholesterol was checked as a young man, it was elevated. Despite my strong family history of early cardiovascular death, I denied these symptoms . . . because to acknowledge them would require acknowledging the underlying problem. I was *fat*. Until I finally faced up to and combated my own weight problem, I avoided blood pressure cuffs and bathroom scales like the plague.

Still, these physical effects were nothing compared to the psychological trauma of being a fat kid and then a fat adult, and that trauma is still with me today, although the scales say otherwise. My battles against self-consciousness, insecurity and inferiority began in childhood. They were probably at their worst in junior high school, when everything is changing. At this age, kids are labeled by their peers, even their parents. There's the smart kid, the jock and the popular kid. My role, of course, was the fat kid. Deep inside, I still carry that label today.

Fat kids were the minority when I was growing up, but today more children than ever before are living with this stigma. The problem of childhood obesity has never been worse . . . at least one-third of all young people are now overweight.[2,3,4] Yet, despite this growing problem, no meaningful solutions have been offered. Now that I have discovered a solution, I hope to change that. I have made it my mission to separate those two words—*fat* and *kids*—forever.

My Path: How I Discovered the Solution

Not long ago, I had resigned to being forever fat. I had tried everything. I'd read all the books on nutrition, heart disease, obesity and exercise. I'd jog every day, starve myself, lose a few pounds, get really excited . . . and then gain it all back, and then some! When I felt really desperate, I even considered those canned liquid diet supplements. I knew they were useless, and in some cases even dangerous, but I was desperate. Still nothing worked.

I had to make a choice. One possibility was a life of monastic deprivation, denying myself all the culinary joys that I had ever experienced combined with five miles a day on the treadmill. Or I could accept being fat—forever—and continue partaking of the things in life that gave me joy. Realizing that my wife and I were raising two children, with trips to Disney World, birthday parties, fast food and all the rest, the life of a monk simply was not going to happen. And since one of the few rewards we give ourselves is an occasional night out at a nice restaurant, there was not much we could renounce without eliminating the joy of life altogether.

So I threw in the towel. Getting thin was beyond me. There was a force behind this problem that was beyond my comprehension or my control. If I couldn't help myself, how could I possibly help the kids in my practice who suffered from obesity?

Then one day my being fat became more than a cosmetic concern. The blood pressure and cholesterol problems I had always ignored finally caught up with me. On a routine insurance physical shortly after my forty-second birthday, my cholesterol was 300 and my blood pressure was 150/90. Although I am only five-feet nine-inches tall, my weight had ballooned to two hundred pounds. I was forced to accept reality. Not only was I still fat, but I was also officially unhealthy. Now I *had* to do something—but what?

My wife, the guiding light of my life, is a former pediatric critical-care nurse. She has never been interested in TV talk shows, but one day she overheard an interview about obesity. Two very popular diets were being compared. One was the well-known "Zone" program,[5] and the other *The New Beverly Hills Diet,* written by my coauthor Judy Mazel. This was an updated and revised version of *The Beverly Hills Diet,* first published in 1981, which pioneered the concepts of food combining for weight loss and weight maintenance, as well as the use of natural enzymes to achieve lifelong slimhood.[6] Judy talked about the role that enzymes had played throughout history, dating back to China's *Classics of Internal Medicine of the Yellow Emperor* (2598–1606 B.C.). The ancients relied on these principles not for weight control, but to promote proper digestion.

Judy impressed my wife. Her ideas were clear and reasonable. Although the principles of the Beverly Hills Diet were different from anything she had been taught in nursing school, her instincts told her that what Judy said made sense.

That night my wife told me about what she'd seen on television and said she wanted us both to read Judy Mazel's book. More importantly, she had decided that we were both going to start the diet on Monday. Since I had all but given up on ever losing the weight I knew I had to lose, I figured I had nothing to lose trying. Besides, my wife's enthusiasm was infectious.

What followed changed my life. The diet proved incredibly successful for both of us. In just over a month, I lost twenty pounds. We continued on the maintenance program and kept losing weight. Best of all, there was no deprivation! Throughout the process we became educated about the principles of food combining and natural enzymes, the hallmarks of Judy's method.

The New Beverly Hills Diet was fun, and it was *healthy*. Each day began with delicious fruits, some of which I had never tasted before, such as luscious mangoes and succulent papaya. We also ate corn on the cob, baked potatoes, and even steak and shrimp during the first week. We felt better, more energetic, vibrant and alive than we had felt in years. We were losing weight by eating responsibly without restricting the nutrients our bodies needed. Unlike traditional diets, we weren't losing weight by starving our bodies; we were losing weight by feeding them. We didn't count calories or fat grams. We didn't take food supplements or eliminate entire food groups such as fats or carbohydrates. And for the most part, we ate natural foods, as free as possible from chemicals and preservatives.

Quite by accident, we had found "the answer" . . . the miracle we had been waiting for . . . a way of eating that allowed us to enjoy food, eating, good health and slimness. There was no question that Judy Mazel had discovered the solution to the obesity problem.

A Revelation: Could This Work for Children?

Almost immediately it occurred to me that *The New Beverly Hills Diet* could be adapted for children. After all, it worked: it was healthy and no food groups were restricted. The food was natural and full of nutrients. Above all, it was *safe*. Children should not be placed on diets, in the traditional sense, nor should major food groups be restricted. *The New Beverly Hills Diet* offered a well-rounded eating plan for a lifetime, and for the whole family. It was perfect for the growth and high energy requirements of children.

True, the diet's concepts of food combining and reliance on natural enzymes to promote efficient digestion were counter to everything I'd ever learned in medical school or residency. There, we had been brainwashed by the doctrine of modern organized eating, our current three-meal-a-day plan, a concept based on false information and misconceived ideas that have led to the obesity epidemic. *The New Beverly Hills Diet* forced me to rethink all these traditional concepts, to learn a way of eating that not only promoted slimness, but that was also healthier than the three square meals a day I'd grown up on.

Finally, I decided to write to Judy to tell her how profoundly her book had affected me. The last thing I expected was a reply from the author whose book had topped the *New York Times* bestseller list.

But answer me she did. In a follow-up call, I discovered she shared my passion for solving the problem of childhood obesity. She was thrilled to learn that her concepts could be applied to kids. From my standpoint as a pediatrician and as a parent, I was certain Judy's method could change the lives of children just as it has done for millions of adults.

TWO

Just Who Are
These Fat Kids?

There Are More Fat Kids
Than Ever Before, and the Numbers
Are Growing

The statistics are staggering. One in three children is over-weight, if not actually obese, and the numbers continue to grow. It is estimated that in the last twenty years, obesity has increased 54 percent among children six to eleven and 39 percent among children aged twelve to seventeen.[7]

Despite the statistics, childhood obesity remains very difficult to define, even by the experts in childhood nutrition and weight control.[8] Part of the difficulty lies in how the term is defined. Taber's *Medical Dictionary,* defines *obesity* as "an abnormal amount of fat on the body. Term usually not employed unless individual is from 20–30 percent over average weight for his age, sex and height. Obesity is the result of an imbalance between food eaten and energy expended, but the underlying cause usually is quite complex and difficult to treat."[9]

Nelson's Textbook of Pediatrics, the "bible" for most pediatricians, hedges a little when it comes to defining obesity. The book declares that there is "no exact line of demarcation" between the obese and nonobese child, and that "practically, the diagnosis is made from the appearance of the child" rather than an arbitrarily set number of excess pounds.[10] Tables and graphs may be helpful, Nelson's goes on to say, but fat is basically in the eye of the beholder.[11,12]

Treating obesity is more of a clinical rather than statistical problem. Because the "overnutrition" of obesity tends to fuel increased height, fat children are generally taller than other kids the same age. Facial features often appear small and fine in relation to full, chubby cheeks. Excess fat tissue often gives boys the appearance of developing breasts. The abdomen in both boys and girls may be large, sometimes hanging over the belt. The external genitalia of boys may appear inordinately small, sometimes prompting a visit to the pediatrician, when in fact the problem is simply that the penis is embedded in fat. The upper arms, thighs and buttocks accumulate excess fat and, in extreme cases, can even show stretch marks. Extremely overweight children can even have gait disturbances because of the stress of increased weight on their legs and hips. The presence of these characteristics confirms the diagnosis of obesity.

Then there are those children who are just plain fat (though not obese). Too often, their parents, teachers and pediatricians dismiss their weight as "normal for this child" or "not overweight for his height" or with some other rationalization. Tell that to those kids' peers who don't need height/weight charts to recognize when a kid is fat—and they refer to him or her accordingly.

The Growth Chart: What Does It Really Tell Us?

When it comes to assessing childhood obesity, the growth chart is a misleading tool. Because children are taller and fatter than ever before in the history of Western civilization, today's kids have simply outgrown the growth curves.[13,14]

In 1966, and then again in 1979, the National Center for Health Statistics compiled data on a huge pool of children of all different ages. They established norms based on this data. When you look at a growth chart, you see a bunch of wavy lines (see next page). The centerline represents the 50th percentile. In other words, for that particular age, 50 percent of children's weights (in 1979) were above the line and 50 percent were below.

Today, twenty years later, the chart has no validity because kids have gotten both taller and progressively heavier. They have, in effect, moved up the growth curve so that the 50 percent line no longer represents 50 percent of the population. Based on data compiled over twenty years ago, the average weight for a one-year-old child was twenty-two pounds, but today the "average weight" is probably much closer to twenty-five pounds. That means that the new average for today's kids is what was once regarded as the 90th percentile.

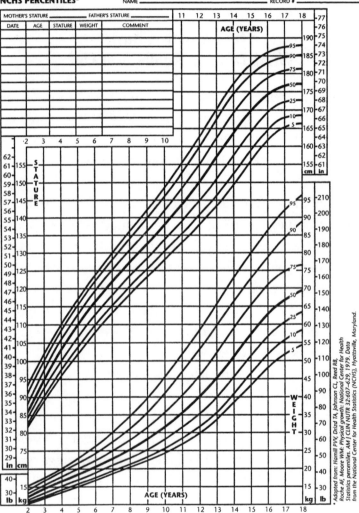

A study done at the University of Chicago in 1996 compared the growth curves of 897 infants at birth, three months, six months and nine months. Compared to the standard charts, the *average* weights of these children were significantly higher than what the growth charts would have predicted.[15]

To complicate this misinterpretation even further, parents view these growth charts as an "exam" to be passed. A very important portion of the "well-child" exam, especially during the first few months of life, is plotting the child's weight on the growth curve. For most parents, this is the high point of the "well-baby" exam, the part they tell their friends about the next day at work. In our goal-oriented world, parents compare their child's progress on the growth chart and use the results as an objective score of their parental success. In fact they, like my wife and I once did, often don't feel they have succeeded unless they "score" at least 90 percent. In our well-meaning innocence, we push to get our infants into that 90th weight percentile, not even realizing that we are setting the stage for obesity, a condition that will haunt the child for the rest of his or her life.

Earlier, when I said kids are bigger than ever before, I did mean "bigger," not just heavier. Prior to puberty, the fattest kids are also the tallest. This is why height for weight charts are inaccurate. An overweight child may appear "normal" for his excessive height, when in fact he is in a state of obesity. A pediatric obesity specialist told one of our Slim & Fit children currently using our program that her weight of 95 pounds was not really a serious problem because she was four-feet tall. It didn't seem to matter to the doctor that the girl was only five years old!

Experts now realize that the growth charts no longer represent reality, but how do you think they propose to solve the discrepancy? A massive public health campaign to bring children's weight back into line? *(Of course not!)* Instead, in the works are new growth charts based on today's data . . . data that even the surgeon general says represents an epidemic of childhood obesity. In effect, we are condoning obesity by redrawing the growth curves to accommodate it! This is kind of like lowering the reading requirements in public schools so that fewer children appear illiterate. Changing the growth curves will certainly disguise the national obesity epidemic. But there will still be just as many fat kids with just as many psychological, sociological and medical problems.

A similar phenomenon occurred several years ago when adults' weight no longer correlated to existing charts prepared by a well-known insurance company. The company's solution was simply to revise the charts, allowing for higher weights at given heights. This was simply giving in to the perception that being overweight or even obese was somehow the natural condition of humanity.[16] When the new charts were criticized as giving adults implicit permission to be fat, public opinion forced the company to return to the original charts. But that sleight of hand hasn't made obesity disappear.

The Problem with Newborns

Newborns have also gotten bigger.[17] While debate continues about whether average birth weight has changed substantially over the last twenty years, there's no debate that the extremes at both ends of the spectrum have become more extreme. There are more big babies, and more tiny ones. Through the miracle of neonatal ICU, more acutely premature babies weighing less than two pounds are surviving than ever before. They represent one end of the spectrum. At the other end of the spectrum are the "giant" babies weighing in at ten, eleven and even twelve pounds. Twenty years ago, an eight-and-one-half-pound baby was considered quite large. Now these babies are commonplace.

Proof in point: My staff and I looked at all the newborns born during an entire week in the greater Tampa area. We found that 30 percent were over eight pounds. . . . 15 percent were over nine pounds . . . and 5 percent of them were over ten pounds!

The problem, however, is not so much that children are starting out bigger, but that they are growing at record-breaking speeds. For centuries, the norm has been for children to double their birth weight in five months and to triple it in a year. Seven-pound babies, therefore, would weigh fourteen pounds at five months and twenty-one pounds on their first birthday. But today's seven-pound baby is likely to weigh fourteen pounds in just three and a half months, and thirty pounds in a year.

What's causing this "Big-Baby" boom? It seems the experts haven't a clue. The average person might explain it as "evolution," but in one generation? The only thing that has evolved, besides our eating patterns, is the use of chemicals, preservatives, steroids and growth hormones in our foods. This is particularly true in meat, chicken, milk and other dairy products. I am worried that these chemicals may not only play a dramatic role in childhood obesity, but also I can't help but wonder if these substances, particularly the hormones added to foods, aren't also affecting the unborn fetus.

"You are what you eat" is an overused cliché, but it is still quite true literally and figuratively. The human body is composed of nutrients, vitamins, minerals, amino acids, glucose, lipids and water. Nutrients are the byproducts, the results of the foods we eat. Nutrients are converted into our flesh and blood and energy. Just as a car can only run on gasoline, our bodies can only run on nutrients. If you put soda pop into the gas tank of your car, it would stay there, stored and unused. Just as a car cannot convert soda pop into energy, our bodies cannot convert chemicals into nutrients. Since they are not nutrients, they are neither utilized nor eliminated, but stored in the cells, tissues and organs of our bodies.

Hence, the additives tainting our food are stored in our bodies, becoming part of us, adding to our weight and, in the case of pregnancy, part of our unborn children. What role do these chemicals play in the developing fetus? Despite the absence of hard medical data, might it not be possible that these chemicals and hormones are playing a role in the increasing birthweight, as well as the rapid growth patterns, of newborns?

Three

What Science Says About Childhood Obesity

The Current State of Research: Getting Help from the Experts

Nutrition has never interested me much. Like most physicians, I spent the mandatory few weeks during biochemistry in medical school learning the basics of carbohydrate, fat and protein metabolism, memorizing it for exams, and then essentially forgetting about it. In practice, when I needed advice about nutrition for my patients, I relied on what the nutritionists at the hospital told me. This makes it very easy for physicians to avoid confronting nutritional issues face to face. What I could not ignore, however, was the growing numbers of severely overweight children.

When I discovered *The New Beverly Hills Diet,* I realized I had stumbled upon a possible cure. That cure lay in working with the digestive system, by using the enzymes found naturally in foods, and by avoiding foods with chemicals, preservatives and hormones.

I decided to see what the scientific community had discovered about childhood obesity by reviewing the medical literature. Although the volume of research was immense, the same basic themes and solutions keep repeating themselves over and over again.

What I learned from hours of research at the medical library can be summed up in a few observations: There are more fat kids than ever before. Childhood obesity leads to many other health problems. Fat is bad and can kill us. Protein is good and will make us live forever. Kids do not exercise enough. Kids watch too much TV. Fat parents have fat kids.[18,19]

Nowhere in my research was there one mention of enzymes or food combining, and the ways in which these can be combined to promote proper digestion.

Obviously Judy Mazel's research does not reflect mainstream science. Most doctors refuse to accept enzymes and food combining as serious approaches to obesity.[20] Despite the millions of dollars that have been spent on grants for research (many sponsored by the food industry), the experts have never been able to take a fresh, unbiased look at ways to solve the epidemic of childhood obesity.

One day, while researching this book on the computer, I came across a new definition for childhood obesity. It made me sad to think that this was all the advice that could be offered to parents desperately seeking solutions to one of life's most frustrating problems.

Obesity exists when your child's weight is 20 percent or more above that considered normal for height. Obese children are usually large at birth and gain weight rapidly. The tendency to gain weight is probably inherited. Most obese children are born with an excess of fat cells and an increased ability to store fat. Appropriate health care includes ruling out certain endocrine problems, treating underlying health problems and establishing life-long good eating habits. Patience, determination, high motivation and a good sense of humor are constant requirements for successful treatment.[21]

I didn't know any fat kids who found their obesity a laughing matter.

Food Combining May Not Have Scientific Endorsement, but It Works

In 1981, Judy Mazel wrote *The Beverly Hills Diet* based on the concepts of conscious food combining and the way that enzymes appearing naturally in foods aid digestion. This philosophy is the cornerstone of the Slim & Fit eating program. (For more details, see part II, section i, "Eating Slim & Fit.") When food is improperly or inefficiently digested, it's stored in the body instead of being metabo-lized. Undigested food turns into fat. To avoid "mal-digestion," foods should be eaten in certain combinations to optimize the activity of our digestive enzymes. Because many fruits contain natural digestive enzymes, fruit is eaten first thing in the morning every day.

What exactly are enzymes? Technically, they are bio-catalysts, chemical reactors that turn food into nutrients. They are what transforms a burger and fries into vitamins and minerals. Individual enzymes perform very specific digestive functions.

Specific enzymes work on specific food groups. Not all enzymes are compatible. In fact, many are antagonistic to one another if foods are taken together in the wrong combinations. Certain combinations of foods can render specific enzymes inactive. In medical school, we studied the Krebs citric-acid cycle, the series of enzyme reactions by which carbohydrates, fats and proteins are digested into carbon dioxide, water and energy. By using the food combining recommended in *Slim & Fit Kids,* we make the Krebs cycle more efficient at burning nutrients as energy rather than storing them as fat.

I am a practitioner, not a researcher, and I acknowledge the need to subject these theories to solid basic scientific research. But my practice puts me on the front lines of the obesity problem and the full force of its destructiveness. And from where I stand, "Conscious Combining" and the use of natural enzymes is safe and practical. I have used these theories myself. Based on my experience, and with full confidence, I urge anyone with weight problems to do the same. Time is of the essence, and to wait for the wheels of traditional experimental science to prove what everyone who is following this style of eating has already proved would lead to unacceptable delays in attacking this problem. If you don't believe me, just ask the fat kids!

The time has come to take up the crusade against childhood obesity, to save the millions of kids who are fat and whose mental and physical health is suffering because of it. It's time for the research community to subject Mazel's theories to the rigors of scientific investigation to determine if these unorthodox principles actually have scientific validity. We are at a point in this battle where all avenues of hope must be investigated.

Four

Fat: What It Is and What It Isn't

Part I: Myths About Weight Gain

Heredity: It's All in the Genes

Tremendous effort has been expended in trying to blame parents' genetic makeup for the fact that children are getting fatter. Recently, scientists have located genes that they feel contribute to some people's propensity toward obesity.[22] But, like all nature versus nurture arguments, we will never be able to blame the entire obesity problem on DNA. Although it is true that DNA plays a role in body type (broad shoulders, long legs, small frame, etc.), fatness isn't a body type. It's a condition, an end result. We're fat because of what we put in our mouths. Fat parents have fat kids because they eat the same foods in the same ways.

Scientists are counting on genetic research to come up with a drug that will allow us to eat whatever we want and never get fat. Just like FenPhen. That was a "miracle pill," a quick fix that resulted in the tragedy of irreparable heart damage. Doesn't it make more sense to experiment with altering the ways we combine our food à la Mazel rather then popping a pill that could be life threatening?

A good example that genetics is not the complete answer to why we get fat comes from looking at married couples. Common sense tells us that husbands and wives have no genes in common, but many grow to resemble each other in body type after years of eating the same things in the same way. It's their dining habits, not their DNA that they share in common.

My biggest concern about concluding that obesity is pre-determined in our DNA is that it will encourage us to blame it on our genes and simply give in to being fat. Although genes determine everything in the body (and therefore undoubtedly play some role in the phenomenon of fat), we must not lose sight of the fact that parental habits are passed down to children just as easily as chromosomes. We may not be able to change our genes, but we *can* do something about the way we eat!

Is It in the Glands?

When you bring your child to a pediatrician because he or she is overweight, the first course of action is to order a medical work-up to determine if there's a medical basis for the weight problem. Endocrine (glandular) abnormalities like hypothyroidism or Cushing's disease can sometimes lead to obesity. These, however, are very rare; in fact, less than 1 percent of overweight children have an endocrine or metabolic explanation for their weight problem. These are not only rare, but also often easily diagnosed by history and physical examination alone. They are also usually treatable.

Is It Evolution?

Are children taller and fatter simply because we are evolving into a larger species? Not if you understand Darwinian theory. According to Darwin, species evolve in response to a threat to their survival. Apart from resulting in more NBA and NFL players, taller and fatter offers us no survival advantage. Becoming giant people instead makes us sicker and more prone to early death.

Is It Lack of Exercise . . . Yes or No?

When it comes to exercise, we are a culture of paradoxes. There are health clubs on nearly every street corner in every major American city, and more Americans than ever before taking part in regular aerobic exercise. Likewise, despite more organized sports activities for children than ever before, children are weaker and have less endurance than ever before. We are, in fact, a society obsessed with exercise and athletics, running to health clubs, sporting events and sporting goods super stores, yet when we return to our homes and offices from these temples of sweat, we are more sedentary than ever before in human history. Naturally, this is also true for children.

Even after watching the explosion of industries spawned by this obsession with exercise (many of whose leaders happen to be overweight), it's obvious that increased exercise *alone* doesn't even come close to solving the obesity problem. True, it builds muscle strength, coordination and agility, and nourishes the feeling that people's minds are more closely connected to their physical selves, and it is vital to the development of a healthy mind and body, which Mazel refers to as the narrowing of the "mind-body split." Losing weight and building self-esteem has a much better chance of success if it is coordinated with a program of exercise designed to heal this split. (See part II, section ii, "Thinking Slim & Fit" and part II, section iii, "Moving Slim & Fit.")

Then if it's not lack of exercise, if we are in fact exercising more than ever before, what is it? What has changed in the last twenty, fifty and one-hundred years is not necessarily exercise, but *movement*. Twenty years ago, children came home after school and played outside for two or three hours until dinner. They participated in sustained, muscle-flexing activity, using all parts of their bodies, and they did this without even realizing the good they were doing themselves.

Even adults move far less than they once did. Years ago people walked where they needed to go and performed more manual labor as part of everyday living. They shoveled snow without snow blowers. They mowed lawns without self-propelled lawn mowers. They trimmed weeds by hand and scrubbed floors on their hands and knees. Elbow grease was our most valued natural resource. Now we rely on our brains rather than our brawn, and our bodies are far less active than they once were. The exercise industry has moved in to try to fill the activity void. Ironically, today we live in a culture where we pay money to drive to the health club to exercise, then pay someone else to do our gardening!

Is It Due to TV?

The much-maligned television set has for years taken the blame for the rise in childhood obesity. Some even blame the remote control! Watching TV is not a new phenomenon, yet childhood obesity has soared just in the last twenty years. Studies tell us that children watch more TV than ever before, but these must be taken with some skepticism. After all, kids are busier than ever before, especially since they also have computers, video games and Gameboys.

Of course, television and obesity are not entirely uncon-nected. True, children are sitting and watching rather than running and playing, but, there is some credence to the argument that time in front of the TV is the *perfect* time for ingesting unhealthy, fat-producing snacks. As someone who consumed many a bag of potato chips in front of *Andy Griffith* and *Gilligan's Island* reruns, I know that part of the joy of mindlessly watching TV is crunching something in your mouth. The beauty of the *Slim & Fit Kids* plan is that it's still possible to munch, watch and grow slender.

Is It the Fat We Eat?

It's time we finally clarified the role of fat in nutrition and in obesity. It amazes me that with all we've read about fat and diets, no one has taken the time to clarify the distinction between fat as a vitally important nutrient and the fat listed on food packages. It's the latter that's actually making us fat.

We have been brainwashed by the no-fat and low-fat food industries, which have become huge and powerful, both in food production and in the information that they distribute. Once Madison Avenue got into the equation, the advertising industry saw an opportunity to capitalize by convincing people that all fat is bad, and to create products that replaced fat with *indigestible* chemical substances.

All the industry had to do was convince parents, health-care workers and educators that if children eat "low-fat" foods, they will have less chance of becoming fat adults. Once this myth was firmly embedded in the national psyche, the brainwashing was complete.

If you doubt that this thinking has pervaded every aspect of modern American life, just watch TV for an evening. Count how many times fat content is mentioned when advertising a food item. Go to the grocery store. Notice that there is a low-fat and no-fat alternative for almost every product on the market, especially those designed for kids. We, as a society, are now eating less fat than ever before, yet we are fatter than ever before. In our folly and naïveté, we are depriving our bodies of a much-needed nutrient.

By restricting fats, we hurt our children by potentially stunting their growth and retarding their development. By restricting *fat calories,* we actually restrict *nutritional fat.* That's right, everyone needs fat. But kids need it even more. Why? Because their nervous, endocrine and immune systems are all developing. If you think you are fulfilling nutritional needs by counting fat content on the side of boxes, you are wrong. Those numbers don't tell us about the nutrient fat, they just happen to use the same terminology. Let me explain.

Fats, or "lipids," are composed of fatty acids. The body can produce some, but not others. The so-called essential fatty acids—linoleic and oleic acids—can only be obtained from the foods we eat. They are vital to good health and the development of young bodies.

Because they are essential to the development of cell walls and internal cell structures, fetal and newborn brains, and nervous and immune systems, they are vital to good health. Fats are also essential components of many important hormones. Essential fatty acids must also be present for the proper metabolism of other body fat tissue. Without them, total body fat may actually increase. What about lecithin, another substance not produced by the body? Like the essential fatty acids, it can only be obtained from the foods we eat. Lecithin is crucial to the development of the nervous system, particularly the neuronal sheaths necessary for nerve conduction and in maintaining acceptable cholesterol levels.

When we parents count fat grams on the sides of the boxes of all the prepared foods we buy, what exactly are we doing? While we are counting and restricting fat calories, we are ignoring the value of *nutritional fat* in the diet. In other words, by restricting total daily fat grams, we also restrict vital nutrients—the essential fatty acids—that are absolutely necessary for normal growth and development.

If this is still confusing, don't worry, because the *Slim & Fit Kids* plan does not count fat grams at all. Instead, it minimizes potentially harmful hydrogenated fats present in processed foods. With a proper balance of all the other food groups, and the inclusion of foods containing nutritional fat, *all fats* will be metabolized effectively without leading to increased body fat.

Is It Too Many Calories?

What actually is a calorie? Technically a kilocalorie, or calorie, is a unit of heat energy produced when a nutrient is burned. When one gram of carbohydrate is metabolized, four calories of energy are produced. Proteins also produce four calories per gram. Fats, the great hoarder of energy, produce nine calories when one gram is metabolized. So, contrary to what the food and diet industry would like you to believe, we do not actually "eat" calories. When we ingest nutrients we do not ingest energy, we ingest "potential" energy, which becomes energy once it is metabolized.

When we store nutrients rather than burn them to produce calories (energy) efficiently, we become obese. Inefficient metabolism, which does not happen when you practice conscious combining, results in storage of nutrients and when too many nutrients are stored, obesity results.

This is why the Slim & Fit eating program does not rely on calorie counting for weight reduction. The calories of *potential* energy that we consume may not reflect the numbers of *actual* calories that are being produced and the amount of undigested food that is stored. It's time to free ourselves from the equation of balancing the number of calories we consume against how many we burn. What we actually eat is food that breaks down into nutrients and is burned for fuel as a calorie. The answer to our national weight problem lies in better understanding, and hopefully controlling, this burning process, the metabolic stage of digestion, and not in counting calories before they have even become calories.

Part II: What Actually Causes Weight Gain?

Our National Obsession with Protein

As a society we are obsessed with protein, and I believe we eat far too much of it. That's a reason many kids are overweight. Kids under age three only need about one gram of protein per pound per day, older children and teenagers *need half that.*[23] Given the content of protein in a Western diet, these are extremely easy requirements to meet.

An important aspect of our eating plan is that protein is very difficult to digest compared to carbohydrates and fats. When present in significant quantities, protein not only slows down, but also blocks the digestion of carbohydrates and fats, leading to undigested food and obesity. *Proper digestion* is the key to being slim.

Even *The American Academy of Pediatrics Guide to Your Child's Nutrition*, a home nutrition reference, declares that "protein is so abundant in the foods Americans eat, that most of us, children and adults alike, consume more than we need. Protein overload may be a more serious problem than protein deficiency."[24]

Despite this, we keep hearing that we need more protein. In fact, the current "pop" trend in dieting is to push protein.[25] When asked what should make up a balanced diet, even my kids say that protein is good and fat is bad. And they add that you can't ever get too much protein. Tell that to the kidneys of America, bombarded with all that urea nitrogen and creatinine to metabolize.

Our bodies are exquisitely designed to burn nutrients for fuel in a very specific way. Carbohydrates are the main fuel source. When they are depleted, the body chooses fats next, the one nutrient designed specifically for storage and reserve energy. When fats are depleted, protein, the body's main structural component, is used, but only when severe depletion of carbohydrates and fats occur, a state commonly known as starvation or *ketosis*. Because protein for energy is primarily used to build cellular structures—not to create energy—metabolizing protein for energy is an incredibly inefficient way for the body to produce fuel.

People who go on high-protein diets are, in fact, starving themselves, which is why they are so successful in losing weight in the short term. But it's downright dangerous for the long term.

When the body metabolizes fats and proteins in the absence of essential carbohydrates, toxic byproducts are produced. These byproducts are known as ketones or ketone bodies. When these build up to a high enough level in the body, an abnormal state known as *ketosis* is created. Those on high-protein diets desire ketosis, although it is abnormal and unsafe. They can tell by the way they feel, in fact, that they are going into ketosis because they feel a "high," and when they feel this "high," they know their high-protein diets are effective. In actual fact, this feeling heralds the beginning of a state of starvation.

Physiologically, ketones behave very much like psychotropic drugs. At low levels, they create a sense of euphoria—the ketotic "high" well known to high-protein dieters. At high levels, they produce sleepiness and disorientation. At even higher levels, coma can result.

Diabetics who receive insufficient insulin can get into this state quite quickly. The coma seen in newly diagnosed diabetics is due to extreme ketosis, combined with the acidosis produced when the body goes too long without sufficient carbohydrates.

The difference between diabetics and high-protein dieters is that diabetics actually consume carbohydrates, but because they lack the insulin to drive glucose into the cells, they replicate starvation on a cellular level. The result is a breakdown in fats and proteins producing ketosis, which can lead to the so-called diabetic coma.

Obviously, untreated diabetes represents the most severe example of carbohydrate deficiency. Yet, it is important to realize that high-protein, low-carbohydrate diets can also produce ketosis harmful to the brain and central nervous system. Many who have tried these fad diets have experienced the light-headedness and occasional fainting associated with this unhealthy approach to eating.

To recommend high-protein diets to children and adolescents is unconscionable. *Complex carbohydrates must be the key to every child's eating plan,* as they are with the Slim & Fit plan. They are crucial for the rapid energy production required by active lives and allow for the proper balance of structure and function required by the developing nervous system.

Still the perpetuation of the protein myth continues. Even the mainstream media seems to have fallen victim to the advertising clout of the meat and dairy industries. I feel sorry for parents who must rely on what they read in popular magazines and see on television for their nutritional information. They look upon these sources as authoritative and therefore believe everything they read in them. Should they believe everything they read?

Not long ago *Good Housekeeping* magazine published a very misleading article by a reputable nutritionist stating that there wasn't enough protein in *The New Beverly Hills Diet.* The author said that by concentrating on fruit and carbohydrates, people participating in the diet ran the risk of protein deficiency, scaring readers into thinking that their muscles and organs would begin to break down if they followed the diet.[26] All this hysteria because the diet did not include that wonderful American dietary icon—*meat*—in every meal. It pleases me that at long last even Uncle Sam has given those who choose to be vegetarian "permission." The federal government has recently updated its nutritional guidelines telling us that even vegetarian diets, as long as they are well rounded, provide Americans with more than enough protein to maintain healthy bodies.

Protein Alternatives

While I'm not recommending you or your child become a full-fledged vegetarian, you really need to think seriously about the amount of animal protein you and your child ingest, and start looking for other sources of protein that are easier to digest and will compete less with the digestion of fats and carbohydrates—sources that may, in fact, be healthier than meat, given the insecticides, antibiotics, hormones and fertilizers present in most of the meat products we eat.

Soy, an excellent protein source, could, I think, provide the answer to many of our nutritional problems, particularly those of children. Soy can literally *replace* animal proteins in all areas of diet. In the short term, soy is extremely beneficial in that it provides carbohydrates, calcium and fiber. Over the course of a lifetime, there is evidence that soy offers protection against heart disease, osteoporosis and elevated cholesterol.

The soybean is a recent addition to our agricultural repertoire. It comes to us from the Far East, where it is considered almost sacred by some Buddhist vegetarians. In America, soy is attracting enormous attention because of its amazing versatility as a healthy, nonmeat protein source.

Soy has other advantages, too. It's a great source of natural zinc, an element that's proving more and more important to healthy diet. It contains phytoestrogens, an estrogen receptor blocker, especially important since the estrogens found in meats have been connected to prostate and breast cancer. Phytoestrogens in soy can potentially block the effects of these chemicals and hormones providing protection against the carcinogens found in our other food products.[27] Can soy also lessen the potential growth-promoting influences of these hormones? Ongoing research will hopefully give us the answers to these questions soon.

The National Obsession with Milk

Cow's milk presents some real problems when it comes to dealing with obesity and other nutritional issues in children. Largely because of one of the most massive and successful advertising campaigns in American food-industry history, we've been led to believe that milk may be the most important food in our diet. But we must consider some crucial issues:

Protein Content

Breast milk contains about one gram of protein per one hundred cc's of fluid volume. Cow's milk contains about *five times* that amount.[28] An excess of protein leads to obesity. Because Americans are obsessed with the fat content of milk and its supposed relation to obesity, the milk industry has developed a variety of low-fat products. But growing children crave fat as a nutrient, and low-fat milk doesn't satisfy them. As they drink more, they consume more protein. To excrete the metabolic byproducts of milk protein, more water is required, creating thirst, causing the child to drink even more milk, resulting in a vicious cycle. In our misguided efforts to reduce the fat content in milk, we have overloaded our children with unnecessary protein and calories, making the problem even worse.

Calcium

While cow's milk is an excellent source of calcium especially since it's been fortified with vitamin D for enhanced absorption, it is not the only source.

Children should also get calcium from other foods in their diet like soybeans, poppy seeds, sesame seeds, almonds, oranges, and green leafy vegetables like collard, mustard and turnip greens. Even broccoli, cabbage and bok choy are excellent sources of calcium.

Paradoxically, high–animal-protein diets may actually promote calcium loss.[29,30,31] Dr. Robert Heaney, a calcium researcher at Creighton University, estimates that one fast-food hamburger results in the loss of 23 mg of calcium in the urine[32] because it appears that protein metabolism requires an acid milieu that promotes calcium excretion by the kidneys. With daily requirements for a six-year-old estimated at about 800 mg per day, it's clear that over time excessive protein ingestion could lead to considerable calcium depletion. It may well be that our kids' lack of calcium is partially due to too much protein in the diet.

Recombinant Bovine Growth Hormone

This very controversial topic was widely discussed in the early 1990s, when the FDA looked into its safety.[33] Recently the issue has come up again, as new information has become known.

Dairy farmers discovered that bovine growth hormone, when injected into mature cows, resulted in greater milk yield. Using cow DNA and genetic engineering, they were able to manufacture cow growth hormone in such quantities that it could be given to large numbers of dairy cattle inexpensively.

Consumer groups took issue with this practice, citing data

that these hormones might promote certain types of cancers in older adults. The FDA investigated the matter and granted approval to farmers to administer the hormone after it determined that it was rendered biologically inactive once consumed by humans.

An article in the *New York Times* cited a Canadian study in which milk from cows treated with growth hormone was fed to rats.[34] Nearly 30 percent of the rats who ingested milk from these cows developed antibodies to the bovine growth hormone. The development of antibodies suggests that the hormone *was* biologically active in these rats. Dr. Michael Hanson, commenting on the study, stated, "It is clear that the FDA has misled us."

Soon after this study, Senators Leahy and Jeffords of Vermont, a very important dairy state, contacted Secretary Donna Shalala demanding that the FDA be investigated as to whether certain data was overlooked when reaching their original determination on the use of this growth hormone.

So the issue remains an open one, and my question is this: If recombinant bovine growth hormone has biological activity and may cause cancer, then why couldn't it also do what it was meant to do—cause *growth*—and therefore contribute to excessive growth when taken in by children in large quantities? Or when passed onto unborn babies whose mothers have been drinking the recommended high quantities of milk?

It's time to take a serious look at other alternatives to commercially produced cow's milk, such as soy milk or Rice Dream, a "milk created from rice." Once fortified with calcium, soy becomes a superb alternative to milk. Another alternative is organic milk from cows not subjected to fertil-izers, antibiotics or hormones. Horizon and Altadena Dairies distribute organic milk to major supermarkets nationwide. "Mothers and Others," a New York City organization (212-242-0010), offers consumers tips on how to obtain dairy products from cows not treated with recombinant bovine growth hormone.[35] As the "organic" movement becomes more popular, these alternatives will become more widely accessible and less expensive.

The Role of Sweets

Kids will always eat candy, and there's not much we can do about it. Sugar, the active ingredient in candy, is readily available and very easily digested, metabolized and absorbed. The same can't be said of the preservatives, arti-ficial flavorings and colorings also found in sweets. Most troubling about these additives is that they can't be digested and instead are stored in the body. Like other maldigested substances, they may actually make kids fat.

The sugar in candy is so easily metabolized that, when given the choice, the body would rather break down and absorb this easily obtainable energy source than any other nutrients. Once energy needs are met by the easily metabo-lized sugar in candy, all nutrients and preservatives left behind are stored. If candy makes up a large percentage of your children's diets, they will invariably get fat. They could also become malnourished because there are very few other nutrients in candy other than pure sugar.

High-Sodium Snacks

Sodium is an essential element for life. It is usually found in combination with chloride to form sodium chloride, or NaCl, or table salt. The sodium chloride concentration of our blood is exactly that of the planet's oceans from which all life emerged when the earth was formed. Our body endeavors to maintain this perfect sodium concentration for optimal function by manipulating our water balance.

Imagine taking a glass of water and filling it with table salt. When more water is added, the salt in the glass dissolves. Conversely, when the amount of water in the glass is reduced, salt becomes more concentrated.

In the body, the process works very much the same way. When we consume excessive sodium, either by adding salt at the table or by eating foods already high in sodium, our body hangs on to water by excreting less urine, thereby maintaining the salt concentration at the desirable level. That's what people mean when they refer to "retaining water." Excess salt leads to excess water, which leads to unnecessary weight.

Sodium is in almost everything we eat, especially artificial preservatives like sodium nitrate, sodium sorbinate and sodium propinate. These additives further increase the amount of sodium in the body.

Then there's the astoundingly high levels of sodium in snacks and prepared foods, making the battle against obesity even more difficult to fight. But it is still possible to have plenty of flavor in your food without salt while reaping the benefit of weight loss. In part II, section i, "Eating Slim &

Fit," as well as in Judy's cookbook *The New Beverly Hills Diet Recipes to Forever*, she will show you how to add zest to your diet by *passing* the salt!

The desire for additional salt is an acquired taste. If we never introduce our children to the salt shaker, they would never feel as if they needed to add salt to their foods. But very early on, we expose them to our own bad habits. For example, they learn that many foods—like popcorn or French fries, even eggs—only taste good loaded with salt. In actual fact, rather than enhancing the intrinsic flavor of food, salt disguises it.

Poisons Added to Our Foods

A funeral director friend of mine jokes that with all the preservatives added to our foods these days, soon he won't have to embalm bodies anymore! This black humor is a warning to take seriously. Just what effect do toxins, preservatives and hormones present in so much of today's food?

In his book *Living Healthy in a Toxic World*, David Steinman elucidates this issue concisely.[36] As humans, we are at the top of the food chain. When we eat cattle and chickens raised on feed laced with fertilizers and hormones to increase meat quality, we also eat all of these substances that have been stored in the animals' fat.

Then there are antibiotics added to livestock feed to prevent them from acquiring infectious diseases. While no one would deny the need to keep our commercial livestock disease free, just as we are seeing in human medicine, this indiscriminant use of antibiotics may contribute to the truly frightening increase in resistant bacteria and diseases that are becoming increasingly difficult to treat with our present antibiotics.

The preservatives added to food after it's processed are intended to extend shelf life and keep it "fresh" after you bring it home. This process begs the question: Why, in this age of global rapid transportation and the recent proliferation of mega supermarkets on almost every corner, food *needs* to be preserved for so long? Case in point—sour cream. Until recently, it had no preservatives, yet the product remained unspoiled for a good six months. Now suddenly, preservatives have been added. Do we really need sour cream to last a lifetime? The answer is undoubtedly economic, having more to do with how long a *grocery store* can store food without suffering spoilage.

Food additives are not food nor are they metabolized like food. Exactly what does happen to these chemicals once they are stored in our body tissues? Do they remain in their active forms, wreaking havoc on surrounding cells? Do they affect the way *the fat* in which they are stored is later metabolized? Or, do they simply make our kids and us fat as our bodies become repositories for huge mountains of indigestible, potentially poisonous materials?

In an era where we can use state-of-the-art sanitation techniques, we ought to be able to raise meats and other agricultural products that are disease free and otherwise safe for human consumption without excessive amounts of chemicals and preservatives.

It has never been easier to buy organic "health foods," thanks to the increasing popularity of the organic food movement and growth of large health-food store chains like Whole Foods and Wild Oats. These have made health foods affordable and commercial, so there are now healthy equivalents for virtually everything unhealthy. Shopping at these stores has given consumers accessible alternatives to the rising tide of chemically tainted nonfood.

Could It Be School Lunches?

The mission of the school lunch program is to provide one-third of the daily nutritional needs of children while also providing instruction on lifelong healthy eating patterns. The program has been influenced strongly by nutritionists who insist that the best way to prevent cardiovascular disease in adulthood is to eat low-fat and low-salt foods as a child.

The nutritional theory behind school lunches is the ubiquitous "food pyramid."[37] The basic tenet of the pyramid's organization is that grains and complex carbohydrates are the foundation that we should eat the most of every day. These are located at the widest part of the pyramid, on the bottom.

Two things bother me about using the food pyramid as the basis for school lunches. If milk, meats, fats and sweets are to be de-emphasized, then why are they at the pinnacle of the pyramid, one normally associated with esteem and reverence? Perhaps we should be teaching it as an upside-down pyramid with grains at the top! Also, if meats and dairy are considered of secondary importance to grains, why are meats included almost daily in every lunch? Hard to break away from that great American tradition of meat with every meal, isn't it? Even for the schools.

What really saddens me are the actual menu selections

from which kids must choose. There seems to be a high concentration of foods like corn dogs and "turkey surprise." I'm not saying that kids shouldn't get foods that are fun, but highly processed, heavily lard-laden corn dogs shouldn't be a "regular." When I realized that the federal government, for the purposes of its subsidized lunch program, once classified ketchup as a vegetable, it became clear that their priorities are misplaced.

In 1996, responsible government agencies realized that the school lunch program was not doing its intended job, so it published the "School Meals Initiative for Healthy Children," which made the following recommendations:

1. No more than 30 percent of total calories should come from fat.

2. Vegetables and grains should be emphasized more.

3. A balance of the five food groups should be attained.

4. There should be more vegetarian main courses, less beef and pork and fewer fried foods.[38]

Aside from the emphasis on "fat percentages," these recommendations would go a long way toward improving nutrition, preventing and controlling obesity, and preventing later health problems. The problem is implementing the guidelines.

The good news is that some schools are using rather ingenious tactics to improve the quality of their lunches such as introducing into their programs ethnic foods, such as those from Latin America, Italy, India and the Middle

East. Because of the foods popular in these cultures, more dishes containing beans and legumes as protein sources, along with pasta, rice and other complex carbohydrates can be included in the lunch programs. This has the additional benefit of educating the students about different cultures and different ways of eating.

Many schools are also using soy products more extensively. These are promising first steps. As we discussed previously, soy is a superb protein source that fits well into the Slim & Fit eating plan because of its easy digestibility and wide spectrum of uses, including veggie burgers, soy dogs and soy bologna sandwiches, as well as "Slim & Fit Pure Energy Gourmet Kid Cuisine" (chapter 11), and other imaginative options you'll discover. But, until the school lunch program adapts its own recommendations more extensively and decreases its reliance on meat protein and dairy products as its main course, school lunches will remain a major contributor to the childhood obesity problem.

Five

Feeding and Growing Kids: They Aren't Just Small Adults!

Kids and adults are as different from each other as cats are from dogs. This has been my mantra as long as I have been caring for sick kids. It's what I tell administrators of general hospitals who try to save money by substituting scaled-down equipment designed for adults as stop-gap measures to fill critical shortages in pediatric units. It's equally ineffective to substitute "adult nurses" for those specially trained to care for children.

Likewise, nutrition and weight control for kids is different than for adults. The most obvious physiologic difference between children and adults is that children are still growing and developing. Consequently, "diets" in the traditional sense are inappropriate because restricting calories or limiting food groups can be dangerous to developing young bodies.

Nor should the "no-fat/low-fat" movement so hugely popular with adults be applied to kids. Children need fat—

nutritional fat—but as we have seen, current recommendations seem to categorize all types of fat together. The "good
fat" is absolutely essential to growing bodies and shouldn't
be restricted.

As kids grow, their nutritional requirements, activities and
level of development continue to change. What works for a
two-year-old will not be workable for a thirteen-year-old.
An effective eating plan needs to be flexible and able to
"grow" with the child. To understand these issues a little
better, we will look at each nutritional developmental stage
as a foundation for understanding how our Slim & Fit eating plan will work within each stage, so that you can adapt
it to your child's specific nutritional and emotional needs.

The First Year of Life

Nutrition and growth are practically an obsession with
new parents, as well they should be. The approach to eating
that parents establish for their children during this period
will no doubt set the tone for the rest of their childhood.

The best thing for kids to eat during this age is breast
milk. The protein, fat and carbohydrate content are exactly
what a growing baby's body needs. Formulas were invented
as a substitute for breast milk when breast-feeding was for
some reason impractical or unsuccessful. Although formula
is obviously imperfect because it is artificial, breast milk also
has its drawbacks.

The quality of breast milk, of course, depends on the
nutrition of the mother. If she eats a diet high in chemicals,
preservatives, additives and hormones, these will be passed

along in the milk to the baby with a possibly deleterious effect on the child's growth. Because formula is a manufactured product, it may also contain additives.

Twenty years ago, when I was in medical school, we were taught that the average newborn should double its birth weight in five months, and triple it in a year. Hence, the average seven-pound baby at birth will weigh fourteen pounds by five months and twenty-one pounds at a year. This is also what the growth curves, discussed earlier, reflect. But as we've seen, babies are growing much faster, with many doubling their birth weights in two or three months. Parents mistakenly think that they must be doing a great job since their baby is growing faster than anticipated. Unfortunately, they may not feel quite the same when this accelerated growth velocity continues at age five or six years, resulting in a grossly overweight child.

Some of the explanation for this inappropriate weight gain during the first year may be due to improper food combining in the form of premature introduction of solid foods. Let me explain. In the early part of the century, even as late as the twenties and thirties, children ate nothing but breast milk or some substitute until they were a year old. That's when solids were introduced. By the 1950s, solids were beginning to be introduced as early as the fourth month. Today, very few babies even make it to four months of age without starting cereals, followed a month or two later by fruits and vegetables. By the time they are nine or ten months old they are eating meats and even fast foods. I'm sure you have seen the fast-food–chain ads, specifically targeting young children. Some go so far as to suggest that

Mom bring her baby in to the local fast-food chain to experience his or her first meal!

Why is there this hurry to give kids solid food? There is really no solid scientific evidence that babies need anything other than formula or breast milk during the first year. Some experts suggest that if solids are not introduced early enough, babies may not develop an interest in them. As far as I can tell, this is unsubstantiated. In fact, some pediatricians feel that parents should go back to feeding their children only breast milk or formula as long as possible during the first year of life.

When we discuss the digestive physiology behind the Slim & Fit plan, you'll see that protein and carbohydrates are digested in completely different ways. During the first year of life, nutrients are provided in the form of protein found in milk. When carbohydrates (cereal) are introduced prematurely, they are not digested efficiently because of the effects of the miscombination with protein. Excessive maldigested food leads to excess weight. Relying on milk or formula for a longer period may result in leaner, healthier babies as they emerge from their first year into toddlerhood.

The Second Year: Losing the Baby Fat

By the end of the first year of life, what started out as a primordial, yet beautiful, bundle of potential energy becomes an actual human being. Toddlers walk, babble, laugh, play and pick up all sorts of things and put them in their mouth.

At this stage, children no longer depend exclusively on

breast milk or formula as a primary source of nutrients as their eating experiences greatly widen.

Growth slows down during the second year, as does appetite. Much of the picky eating that toddlers demonstrate is due, to some extent, to the fact that their appetites have considerably diminished. This can cause concern for parents, however, many of whom continue to be in the "all weight gain is good" mode. This, very often, is where the "finish everything on your plate"-syndrome begins.

But this is a time when little bodies are changing. Children lose some of the fat that has made up a large percentage of their body weight for the first nine months of life. They continue to gain height, but at a much slower rate. The result is that their bodies become longer and, *we hope,* leaner.

They also experience tremendous growth in the size and sophistication of their nervous systems. By the end of the first year of life, the brain is about two-thirds of adult size; by the end of the second year, nearly four-fifths of adult size.

Because of this tremendous growth, fats—containing essential fatty acids and compounds like lecithin—are crucial to the development of the nervous system and should never be limited. These, of course, can't be obtained from processed, hydrogenated fats found in most snack foods and low-fat foods.

At one year of age, a child requires one gram of protein per pound of body weight in order to achieve proper growth. Per body weight, this is the highest percentage of protein that they are ever going to require. For example, a twenty-five-pound toddler needs about twenty to twenty-five grams of protein per day in order to sustain proper growth.[39] When a simple slice of bread contains two to four grams of protein, and one glass of milk contains nine protein grams, you can see how quickly this total adds up.[40] In other words, a reasonably balanced diet will provide your toddler with all the protein he or she needs to grow properly.

Watch the way twelve- to twenty-four-month-old kids eat, and you will see that they are natural food combiners. That's why children's plates have dividers. They only *want* to eat one thing at a time. They would really rather just eat their hot dog or their French fries, or their yellow corn separately at one sitting. We teach them to put potatoes and peas on top of meat loaf and mix their foods together in ways that they find totally undesirable.

So if young children want to eat only carbohydrates, let them. The next meal they may want to eat only protein.

You will see as we go on that it is time to get the "balanced meal" concept out of our minds once and for all. We need to begin thinking about fulfilling nutritional requirements over the space of a day, several days or even a week—not at every meal.

My kids, who have always been thin, despite their not-so-thin parents, are natural food combiners. My wife and I would love to accept credit for this, but they did it all on their own. We tried serving them so-called "balanced" meals, but they never ate the entire thing. If we gave them chicken fingers, and tried to add French fries and a vegetable to the meal, they would only eat the chicken fingers. Another time they would just eat the fries and the veggies.

Whatever they chose to eat that meal they would leave the rest, no matter how hard we fought with them.

We can learn much from our children about instincts, basic human drives and behaviors. When they are young, they eat because their body tells them to eat, and if it is available to them, they eat *what* their body tells them to eat. If adults do not pressure them, they rarely miscombine food groups. In my opinion, the proof that food combining works in preventing childhood obesity is that most of the young people who have been allowed to eat instinctually, one food group at a time, remain slim and fit.

The Preschool Years: Their World Expands

These are truly miraculous years. From age three to five, growth is still somewhat slow, but then begins to increase dramatically as school age approaches. Kids' bodies change shape so that they no longer look like little babies. The curved lower back and protuberant belly begin to disappear by about age four and the previously chubby hands and feet take on a leaner, more mature appearance. Their head and facial shape continue to change and even though most of their brain growth has already occurred, there is a tremendous acceleration of intellectual capacity. Their little brains and memory banks take in everything they are exposed to, and language takes on new levels of sophistication.

With the acquisition of new language skills comes the struggle for power with parents. "No" becomes one of their favorite words. Much of this power struggle plays itself out at mealtime. They know what they like, and they are not afraid to tell you. The fussy eating that began to emerge in two-year-olds may become even more militant as the preschool years progress.

Don't push too hard. It is important to try to keep meal-time an enjoyable time. Children will learn early on that meals are no fun if they are always associated with yelling and crying.

Keep in mind that caloric and protein requirements at this age are probably far less than you think. Children at this age may eat almost nothing for breakfast, but rest assured they *will* eventually get hungry, so it is important, when they do finally feel like eating, to have the right food choices available for them.

Once again, don't discount their instincts when it comes to food mixing. Take advantage of it, in fact, by only introducing one new food item to them at a time. Remember that children this age may have to see something on their plate several times before they are willing to give it a try. There may be days when they will eat only a bowl of dry cereal. When this happens, think of good nutrition in terms of an entire week, not one day or one meal. Remember also that even cereal contains protein.

When my son was this age, he existed on pasta with butter and fruit. I was beside myself thinking that if I could not get him to drink more milk or eat more meat he would never grow, or do well in school. Now that he is well beyond that stage, I have been proven wrong. He is growing like a weed and his last report card made me very proud! Possibly, he knew more about the nutrients his body needed than I did.

The Early School Years

Your child now leaves home for long periods every day, interacting with peers, teachers and school lunchroom personnel. This is when children begin to eat more and more of their meals away from home.

Physically, it is a period characterized by steady growth. Since this is also an incredibly active period in a child's life, caloric needs are astronomical. At this age, kids literally "run out of gas" when they have burned up all their available nutrients. To meet this huge need for readily attainable energy, complex carbohydrates must be the mainstay of nutrition. *Breads, rice, pasta and other complex carbohydrates*, as the food pyramid suggests, *must be* the foundation for these kids.

Breakfast presents particular problems during the school-age years. In general, children hate breakfast, and there is very little time in the morning to fight the battles necessary to make them eat! So, very often, breakfast is a Pop Tart in the car on the way to school, or half a glass of reconstituted—not even real—orange juice on the way out the door.

When I was on Judy's diet, I discovered an interesting thing. My children were much more interested in the fruits I was eating for breakfast than the fare we were trying to force them to eat. So I began sharing, and the results were so much more pleasant! Pineapple, mango, a strawberry shake, even watermelon were so much more exciting to them than frozen waffles or cereal with milk. Ironically, because they liked the fruits better, they actually ended up eating more. They were light, tangy, sweet and just what their bodies called for first thing in the morning. Since lunch was then a long way off, we packed them a mid-morning snack of dry cereal or a bagel. This gave them the most efficient energy sources, which supplied them with just what they needed for their busy, demanding school day.

The early school years culminate with the pre-adolescent growth spurt, which these days seems to be occurring earlier and earlier as a direct result of the obesity epidemic. As body fat increases, height increases and the onset of sexual maturity occurs sooner. When sexual maturity occurs sooner, so does sex, which is why I see eleven-year-old girls who are sexually active and mothers at age thirteen. I am also concerned about the use of growth hormones and sex hormones in meat and milk production. Could these substances be adding to an already menacing problem? Certainly more research is needed to answer these questions.

Although excess weight may have started to appear in earlier years, during this phase it can become a full-fledged problem. As school-age children begin to drift away from their parents' control and more into the sphere of influence of their peers, body image becomes more important. This is when kids really begin to notice excess weight, and to pick on those children they perceive as different because they are fat.

This may be the age when parents finally feel compelled to go to the pediatrician specifically for answers on how to deal with their child's weight problem. Although many suggestions may flow from these discussions, definitive answers may prove elusive. Until now, there were no effective solutions to the problem of childhood obesity.

This is tragic for the child, because by the age of seven or eight, much of the psychological damage of obesity may have already been done and will be extremely difficult to undo. How can we avoid it? By being honest with ourselves and recognizing the problem before it becomes extreme. This includes adopting the Slim & Fit method for our families before obesity even hints at becoming a problem.

Adolescents: Young Adults?

Adolescence is a very complex and potentially frustrating and confusing time in the lives of children and their parents. It is a time of endless conflicts and often difficult resolutions. The manner in which teenagers deal with the conflicts they face will shape the way they deal with conflicts and relationships for the rest of their lives.

Adolescents are forced to make decisions based on the values we taught them as younger children. They have to deal with the unavoidable issues of sex, drugs, school work, making money, deciding their futures, complex relationships with peers and the changing relationship with their parents from whom they seek autonomy, but they still crave acceptance. It is perhaps the most traumatic period faced by any human being during their development, and it is made incredibly more difficult if the child must also deal with a weight problem. Hopefully, children have already developed healthy eating and exercise patterns by the time they reach the teen years, but if not, it is never too late to start. After all, look how long it took me to change my ways!

Physically, adolescence continues to be a time of incredible growth, physical and sexual maturation—which, as we've noted, is happening earlier and earlier—and vigorous physical activity that requires huge amounts of nutrient energy. For this reason, *complex carbohydrates should continue to be the mainstay of the adolescent diet, proteins need not be overly emphasized, and nutrient fat must not be restricted.*

Six

Understanding Nutrition and Digestion: The Key to Success in the Slim & Fit Program

The Process of Turning Food into Nutrients

My trusty medical dictionary defines "nutrition" as:

The sum total of the processes involved in the taking in and utilization of food substances by which growth, repair, and maintenance of activities in the body as a whole or in any of its parts is accomplished.[41]

In order to incorporate the Slim & Fit eating method into your children's lives, you must first understand these concepts. At its simplest level, nutrition is the study of how food is taken in, broken down and either burned for fuel, used to build new tissue or stored. In its totality, it is the way in which the food you eat becomes you.

Before we go into any greater detail, let's review a few basic concepts:

1. Food is converted to nutrients by your body. Nutrients—vitamins, minerals, amino acids, glucose, lipids and water—are required in order to sustain life.

2. Enzymes carry out digestion—the breakdown of food into nutrients. Enzymes are tiny proteins that catalyze (promote) chemical reactions. They are produced by the body or are present in the foods we eat.

3. Enzymes have very specific jobs to do and can only function correctly if they are working in the proper environment. There are specific enzymes for the breakdown of each food group—carbohydrates, proteins and fats—and they can only work on their designated food group.

4. Not only do enzymes have specific jobs, but also one enzyme cannot do the job of another enzyme. What's more, the activity of one may actually inhibit the activity of another.

There are literally hundreds of enzymes promoting the millions of chemical reactions that go on in the body each day. Enzymes mediate everything, from controlling blood pressure to metabolizing that Tylenol you took for your headache last night. In order to understand digestion, however, we really only need to focus on a few specific enzymes. They are the key to understanding the digestive process and why our current tendency to mix food groups is so problematic.

The study of enzymes is based on relatively recent discoveries made in the last 120 years. Enzymes themselves were only discovered in 1878; it took almost another fifty years before they were crystallized in the laboratory. Actually understanding how enzymes work only dates back to 1967. New enzymes and their effects continue to be identified even today. Humanity simply didn't know about enzymes when we began to emphasize food mixing in our diets.[42]

The following enzymes are particularly important in digestion:

Ptyalin—One of the components of saliva, ptyalin is an amylase enzyme secreted by glands in the cheek and under the tongue. Its very specific activity is to break down one of the chemical bonds in the molecule that makes up starch in order to break down carbohydrates. Chewing activates it. When your mother told you to chew your food well, she may not have known about ptyalin, but she instinctively knew it was healthy.

Pepsin—This is an enzyme secreted in the stomach, controlled by a stomach hormone called gastrin. Its job is to assist in the breakdown of protein to amino acids in the stomach and small intestine.

Pancreatic amylase—Like ptyalin, this enzyme acts primarily to break down carbohydrates, but it is released by the pancreas rather than the salivary glands.

Lipases—These enzymes, also secreted by the pancreas, act to break down fats in the small intestine.

Although not specifically an enzyme, *hydrochloric acid* is important to mention here. Secreted in quite large amounts by the stomach, it profoundly affects the activity of all the enzymes mentioned above. For example, protein cannot be broken down by pepsin effectively without doing so in an acid environment created by the presence of hydrochloric acid.

To understand how these enzymes work in *changing* food into nutrients we must examine and understand each stage of the process: digestion, absorption, metabolism and elimination.

Digestion: Putting the Enzymes to Work

As food passes from the mouth, to the esophagus, stomach and finally into the intestines, it is systematically broken down into nutrient components that can be absorbed by the small intestine.

In the mouth, the process of chewing activates the production of ptyalin-containing saliva, which immediately begins to break down carbohydrates. Proteins, fats and that unique group of carbohydrates—fruits—pass through the mouth pretty much intact on their way to the stomach.

Once in the stomach, carbohydrates are broken down into carbon fragments, which in turn will finally be broken down by enzymes of the small intestine. This process works in an alkaline environment. Once the stomach becomes acidic, prompted by the presence of protein, it no longer does a good job of breaking down carbohydrates.

The breakdown of fat also begins in the stomach. Fat, in

preparation for its eventual further breakdown and absorption in the small intestine, is softened by acid.

If properly prepared by the stomach, food is finally broken down into its absorbable nutrients when it reaches the small intestine. Stimulated by the presence of fats and partially broken-down carbohydrates the pancreas secretes pancreatic amylase and lipase, which break food down into usable nutrient components. The small intestine, which is many feet in length, absorbs these nutrients and delivers them to the bloodstream.

Fruits are a unique category of food that deserves special mention. Though technically classified as carbohydrates, they are actually in a class all their own. Many contain their own enzymes and do not require action by the enzymes of the mouth, stomach and small intestine to be digested. The breakdown and absorption of fruit occurs so rapidly that the first bites of a pineapple are often being transported into the bloodstream before the entire fruit is even finished!

Absorption

This is the second stage of the digestive process whereby all the cells of the body are ultimately nourished. What started out as a ham sandwich, a box of Chicken McNuggets or a Twinkie is broken down to its most basic, single carbon, amino acid or lipid elements. These nutrients travel through the intestines into the bloodstream, where they traverse miles of arteries, arterioles and capillaries to eventually reach every single cell in the body providing the nutrition necessary for cellular function.

Metabolism

In the third stage of the digestive process, the cells finally get to perform their designated functions, contingent upon the energy and building blocks they receive. This is a vitally important concept. It is the reason why most "diets" don't work. Quite simply, without fuel, the engine won't run. If cells aren't fed, they won't do their jobs. This means energy won't be created, muscle will not be built and enzymes vital to the digestive process will not be manufactured. Most diets restrict food groups so our bodies do not get the 60 percent carbohydrates, 20 percent protein and 20 percent fat needed for proper nutrition, so the body works inefficiently. So-called "slow metabolism" or the feelings of lethargy many people get when they start a diet are simply caused by the body's cells not receiving enough nutrients to metabolize effectively. In essence, they are being malnourished.

Elimination

This is the final stage of the digestive process. Although it seems to be the stage with which most Americans are obsessed, it is probably the least important from a purely nutritional standpoint. Yet, it is critical to weight control—because a pound is a pound no matter how it exists in the body. Inefficient digestion promotes inefficient elimination and constipation, which simply adds to the amount of excess weight carried around.

This is the stage in which nutrients that are not used by the body for energy production or cell building are eliminated along with the waste products of metabolized proteins and carbohydrates. This does not just mean loss through urine and stool. The body also eliminates water, electrolytes and minerals through the skin, and carbon dioxide (a molecule combining unused carbon and oxygen) through breathing. All in all, it is an incredibly intricate and efficient process of utilizing just what the body needs and recycling back to Mother Nature what it no longer requires.

Summing Up

A malfunction along any step of the way can result in a breakdown of the digestive process, resulting in obesity and, in the extreme, malnutrition.

In obesity, the malfunction appears to occur in the first stage of digestion, the stage in which food is converted into nutrients. Quite simply, excess weight results from maldigestion. Sounds like indigestion, doesn't it? As a matter of fact, indigestion and all its associated symptoms— gas, heartburn, cramps, constipation and/or diarrhea—can be a signal that maldigestion has occurred. When food is poorly or inefficiently digested, fat will not be far behind. Excess weight occurs when anything that has been ingested—either foods or "non-foods" such as chemicals, preservatives, and artificial sweeteners—is not digested, absorbed, metabolized or eliminated.

In "Eating Slim & Fit" (part II, section i), we will further explore this concept and how to apply it to our children's lives. First, however, let's take a closer look at key nutritional requirements and their vital importance to the proper functioning of the human body.

Water

Without water, we cannot survive. The adult body is composed of approximately 60 to 65 percent water, while infants' bodies contain 70 to 75 percent. Water plays an integral role in almost every bodily function including all the digestive processes. Many foods, like fruits and vegetables, contain large amounts of water, while proteins contain very little. In order for protein to be digested, large amounts of water must also be consumed. When a person fails to drink enough fluid, water is extracted from the cells of the body resulting in dehydration. This is actually the "weight" people lose on a high-protein diet.

The water shifts that occur each day in the body are astronomical. For example, a twenty-pound infant requires a minimum of one liter (about a quart) of water a day, while the average fourteen-year-old requires two and a half liters to three liters a day. Each day, children lose about 5 percent of their bodies' water in feces, with additional water loss split between evaporation through the skin and urinary losses. When a child suffers from diarrhea or fever, or is exposed to extreme heat, water losses are even greater.

Plain water should become an integral part of your child's diet and should be introduced early in childhood, rather than relying on highly concentrated "fruit" juices and electrolyte drinks loaded with sodium and sugar.

Amino Acids

Proteins consist of twenty-four amino acids, nine of which are considered essential because they cannot be manufactured by the body and must be taken in through the diet. The names of these nine are: threonine, valine, leucine, isoleucine, lysine, tryptophan, phenylalanine, methionine and histidine. The remaining fifteen are considered nonessential because the body can produce them.

Amino acids act as building blocks for all the structures of the body, including muscle, skin, organs, blood and hair. They can be used for energy as well, but only when the body has depleted its carbohydrate stores. In starvation states (ketosis), muscle and eventually organ systems can be affected as protein is broken down for energy.

Glucose

Glucose, derived from carbohydrates, is our ultimate fuel. The production of glucose from carbohydrates is rapid and efficient and the energy obtained almost immediate.

The metabolism of glucose to energy is far more efficient than protein energy. Therefore carbohydrates are obviously a much better energy source than proteins, particularly in children, whose energy demands for both activity and growth are high and immediate.

Lipids

Lipids are the breakdown product of fats and are critical for the growth and development of the human body. Some fatty acids (components of fat) are essential, and must be taken in through the diet. When the amount of such fats is restricted in the diet, the body wants *more of everything else* until the need for these fats is satisfied. In other words, you just want to keep eating. This is one major reason why low-fat and no-fat diets do not keep people thin. More calories end up being consumed just to satisfy essential fat needs. This is also why people can and do consume such large portions when they eat junk foods (processed foods). They *feel* hungry because, while their bodies are consuming fat, it is not natural fat, and they are never truly satisfied.

Vitamins

Quite simply, vitamins are organic compounds that are required in very tiny amounts to assist in certain chemical reactions necessary for growth and maintenance.[43] In other words, they carry on the process of life. In this sense, they are somewhat like enzymes. Without them, the complex functions of the human body cannot be effectively carried out. In a well-balanced diet, sufficient amounts of vitamins carry out the bodily functions successfully. The best source of vitamins is nutritious food, but vitamin supplements can serve as a backup guaranteeing that sufficient amounts of vitamins are ingested.

Minerals

Like vitamins, minerals are inorganic compounds that are necessary to carry on the process of life. Similar to the recent popular interest in vitamins and natural foods, there has been a surge in the interest, research and understanding of the role minerals play in assisting our body in its vital functions. We now realize how important they are as components of a healthy diet. Calcium, magnesium, potassium, sodium, phosphorus, sulfur and chloride are important for normal cellular function. Trace elements like fluorine, copper, zinc, chromium and manganese play important roles in metabolism. Selenium, silicon, boron, nickel, aluminum, arsenic, bromine, molybdenum and strontium are present in most diets and may also be found to play important roles in the body's complex machinery.

Is There Life Without the "Three Squares"?

As a result of our discussion of basic nutrition, I hope you are beginning to understand digestion and the role enzymes play in keeping us slim. The underlying cause of the obesity problem is not what we eat, but how we put together what we eat.

The crux of the problem is that by eating three *square* meals (so called because they contain foods from all the food groups) a day, we combine foods in such a way that much of it is not being digested, absorbed or metabolized efficiently. Every time a square meal is eaten, undigested food is stored. When excessive undigested food is stored, we get fat. It is really just that simple.

So why have we gotten stuck on this ingrained custom of eating all the food groups at once?

In humankind's early years, people ate whenever they were hungry and whenever food was available. Most of the time humans subsisted on nuts and plant products.

Eventually, they learned how to grind some of these products into breads (complex carbohydrates). If they were lucky enough to live in a region where fruit was available, they always had a readily available source of good nutrition and great flavors. They satisfied their yearning for meat only intermittently, when hunting was successful. When it was, they feasted on meat until it was gone. They didn't "round out" the meat with potatoes and vegetables. They ate meat by itself until it was finished or spoiled. Then, they went back to the old staples of fruits, plants and grains.

Eventually humans became more organized and developed farming, from which the concept of land ownership emerged. From this came the need for communities, governments, kingdoms, feudalism, nationalism and of course, war, but that's for another time!

With the advancement of farming, people were able to maintain a constant supply of food. Abandoning the nomadic lifestyle once necessary for the pursuit of food, they began to interact more with their fellow humans. Feasts and festivals with food as the central theme became more popular. Whether it was for celebrating religious festivals, phases of the moon or the bounty of the harvest, breaking bread with friends and loved ones became central to the human experience. Some even celebrated the mere fact that food was available!

Little has changed in terms of the role food plays in modern-day feasts, major holidays and even business negotiations. But our problem today is that we don't only feast when we celebrate, we eat as if every meal is a feast, every day a holiday!

During the late nineteenth century, several simultaneous developments affected the way our culture views food. First, there was the Industrial Revolution. The development of machinery, transportation, production and commerce brought people into the cities. At the same time, science and medical knowledge exploded. Nutrition as a scientific discipline emerged while medicine elucidated the principles of biochemistry and metabolism. But the role that enzymes play in digestion was still not well understood or even considered.

As nutritionists grappled with the tenets of basic nutritional needs, the Industrial Revolution brought about economic pressures for a structured, organized eating plan. Breakfast, lunch and dinner fit very conveniently into the schedule of the factory workday, allowing opportunity for adequate nutrition to be supplied to the masses.

When nutritionists began to formulate their recommendations concerning good eating habits, the concept of three meals had become an economic necessity. To ensure good health, they recommended inclusion of items from all the food groups—carbohydrates, fats, protein and fruits—at each meal. They knew nothing about the effects that combining food groups would have on efficient digestion.

Why, you may be wondering, if people have been combining or "miscombining" food groups all these years, is it only relatively recently that Americans have developed an obesity problem?

To begin with, we no longer eat only three meals a day; we eat all day long! Everything we do and everywhere we go is associated with food. This means that the miscombination of foods occurs all day long. Food never has enough time to fully digest before our system is challenged with even more food. This creates mountains of undigested food that just keeps piling up, making us fatter and fatter.

Then, there's the issue of food quality. The food that we ate fifty years ago was truly food. There were no chemicals, preservatives, hormones or insecticides added. Although there has been a great deal of research into the relationship between these substances and illnesses like cancer, there has been very little, if any, research into how these substances affect digestion and metabolism. Doesn't it make sense that since much of what kids eat today is artificial that there may well be a correlation?

Many nutritionists claim that our increased longevity is a product of our so-called "healthy" diet. Of course, I disagree. Our increased life span has very little to do with "our diet," which is far from healthy; and much more to do with medical breakthroughs like antibiotics, treatment of cardiovascular disease and cancer, advances in critical care and trauma care. Look at the way seat belts, air bags and the awareness campaign concerning the relationship between tobacco and cancer have saved lives. Judging from how widespread childhood obesity has become, how we eat in our culture today may actually contribute more to *disease* than to health and longevity.

Combining Food Groups:
The Crux of the Slim & Fit Plan

This is where our knowledge about food groups, digestion and enzymes comes together. We can now use this information to understand how to combine food groups to promote optimal energy production while preventing obesity.

All foods actually consist of all three nutrient categories. Bread, a carbohydrate, also contains some protein and fat. Even watermelon contains some protein. But when food is broken down into its basic elements, if it is 51 percent glucose, the Slim & Fit plan considers it a carbohydrate, regardless of the other components. If a food consists of 51 percent amino acids, the plan calls it a protein. For the purposes of digestion, a food is considered a member of the food group that is its majority "shareholder." For example, pasta is considered a carbohydrate even though it contains some protein, while meats are considered proteins because they are primarily made up of amino acids.

Here's a quick breakdown of how the major food groups are digested:

Fruits—absorbed almost immediately, they require no bodily enzymes because they contain their own.

Carbs—primarily metabolized by ptyalin secreted in the mouth. A quick source of high energy.

Proteins—require a complicated digestive process that includes hydrochloric acid and pepsin. Take hours to digest.

Fats—not considered when designing your eating program. They are present in all food groups except fruit and are digested in such a way that they will not impede the digestion of the other groups. Besides, we need the nutrient fat, and consequently it is never restricted in this eating plan! The only thing fats can't be combined with are fruits.

Here are simple, easy-to-follow rules of Conscious Combining:

1. Fruit is always eaten alone on an empty stomach for quick absorption. If introduced into the digestive system when other foods are present, it will just sit there, its digestion and absorption essentially blocked by the presence of other foods. It begins to break itself down by rotting, causing gas, indigestion, diarrhea and excess weight gain. Because it is not digested properly, it will turn to fat.

2. Mixing carbs and proteins *should be minimized.* . . . not avoided or eliminated, simply minimized. Once a protein hits the stomach, hydrochloric acid and pepsin are stimulated and the digestion of carbs stops dead in its tracks. Carbohydrates simply cannot be digested once the stomach becomes acidic. Undigested carbohydrates lead to indigestion and ultimately fat.

3. Once animal protein is eaten, it should be followed primarily by protein.

Seven

Fat Can Be Deadly: How Childhood Obesity and Disease Are Related

I frequently hear people say that obesity is not as much a health problem as a cosmetic one. As long as people are physically fit, it doesn't really matter if they are overweight. From my perspective as a critical-care pediatrician, nothing could be farther from the truth. Not only do overweight children have a high risk of becoming overweight adults, but obese children also risk developing medical problems *now,* problems that could have been avoided if they weren't overweight.

Do Fat Kids Become Fat Adults?

Unless something is done during childhood to prevent it, a fat kid will more than likely grow up to be a fat adult. According to statistics, if a child is overweight at age six he or she has a 25 percent chance of going on to become an overweight adult. If children remain fat until they are age twelve, the chances of becoming a fat adult increase to 75 percent.[44,45,46]

Of course, these numbers are not cast in stone. The problem with statistics like these is that they make people feel they have no control over the future. Feeling helpless, they decide that it is impossible for them to help these children avoid becoming obese adults. Since my fat child is going to be a fat adult anyway, they may say, why should we go through the hassle of trying to change his or her life?

Nonsense! With the Slim & Fit plan, fat children can become slim kids and thin and fit adults. But to accomplish these goals, parents have to have the courage to jettison conventional thinking about eating, dieting and digestion.

What have you got to lose? . . . Only the specter of a fat kid growing into an obese adult riddled with health problems that began their dirty work in childhood.

Autopsy studies in young accident victims have demonstrated that the fatty plaques that clog the arteries of many adults are already present in the coronary arteries of young teens.

Hypertension (high blood pressure) can and often does begin in childhood. In very young children, elevated blood pressure is often due to kidney illnesses. But as children grow older and enter their teens, the most common cause of high blood pressure is obesity.

When these overweight teens lose weight, their blood pressure does go down. However, teens with high blood pressure may have already done irreversible damage to the tiny blood vessels supplying organs like the kidney.

Even when these frightening facts are presented to young

people, motivating them to change their lives is extremely difficult. Children and teens believe they are immortal. They believe in the now. The far future is simply an abstraction. That's why we've designed the Slim & Fit plan to be fun rather than a deprivation.

Asthma: Breathing Is a Requirement

More kids have asthma than ever before; even the mortality rate connected to this disease has risen significantly in the last decade. Severe asthma attacks are the most common reason kids are admitted to the hospital.[47]

I have noticed in my practice that an increasing number of asthmatic children are fat and that overweight asthmatics tend to be sicker. Would reducing obesity solve the asthma problem? It would definitely help. Reducing obesity would decrease the severity of asthma attacks and the associated mortality. Here's why:

Asthma is an inflammatory disease. It is triggered by infection, allergies, pollen, toxins and temperature changes, and virtually anything that shocks the lung's small breathing passages, referred to as the lower airways. When agents like these assault the airways, an inflammatory process begins. Fluid, white blood cells and mucus rush to the airways, causing swelling. The tiny layers of smooth muscle surrounding the airways constrict, causing narrowing. Obviously, it's more difficult to force air through narrowed breathing tubes. The characteristic "wheeze" associated with asthma is the result of forcing air through narrowed tubes.

As the airway narrowing progresses, the body experiences

difficulty getting oxygen into the bloodstream and to the rest of the body. To compensate, the respiratory system begins working harder. Asthmatic children breathe faster during an attack as they find it harder to make up for their inadequately functioning lungs.

Here's where fat kids get into trouble.[48,49] First, because they are simply bigger, their bodies require more oxygen, putting additional strain on their heart and lungs. Second, effective breathing requires a functioning diaphragm. With a belly full of fat, the diaphragm has a difficult time descending, which it must do for effective breathing. To assist the function of their diaphragm and chest wall, some kids with asthma have to sleep sitting up just like old people with emphysema.

During restful breathing, we breathe almost exclusively with our diaphragms. When the work of breathing increases during an asthma attack, muscles of the chest wall, shoulders, neck and back must be called into action. When these muscles tire, respiratory failure ensues. Mustering the strength to breathe harder when pounds of extra weight and inches of fat are around the chest, abdomen and back is like swimming wearing weights. You can do it for a while, but eventually you tire and drown.

There are so many different medications now to treat asthma, many of which offer wonderful results. But they are only part of the answer. The Slim & Fit plan to help fat asthmatic kids lose weight is the rest. I am getting tired of seeing severely overweight asthmatic kids with frequent admissions to the hospital, a list of prescriptions as long as my arm and multiple specialists involved with their care, but none of whom are focusing on their most obvious problem—obesity.

Upper Airway Obstruction: Choking on Fat

The reason men my age snore is that their throat and pharynx are flabby. When we sleep, these structures relax and fall into the way of our breathing passages, inhibiting breathing. The snoring sound results when air struggles to get past these collapsed structures.

The same thing happens in obese kids. The problem is much worse if they also have enlarged tonsils and adenoids. Their throat structures, like the rest of their bodies, have become filled with fatty tissue that has no muscle tone and a tendency to flop into the airway, causing blockage. Many of these children receive tonsillectomies in a last-ditch effort to solve the problem. Unfortunately, after they wake up from the anesthesia, they are still fat and their upper-airway obstruction is no better because the underlying problem has not been solved.

Upper-airway obstruction in obese children can actually be quite severe. When breathing passages are blocked during sleep, oxygen levels in the bloodstream drop. Sometimes breathing can cease altogether, resulting in sleep apnea. Usually a child will wake up as a protective mechanism. Occasionally one of these children cannot, and sudden death occurs as the result of obesity.[50]

More commonly, however, upper-airway blockage causes the child to wake up many times during the night, resulting in poor sleep, lethargy and anxiety. During the day the child is easily distracted, unable to concentrate and occasionally hyperactive. Some researchers have postulated that many children have been treated with Ritalin for hyperactivity when in fact their behavior is a result of sleep deprivation caused by obesity—related upper-airway obstruction.

Diabetes: Not Just the Kid's Type Anymore

Diabetes is a tough disease. In most cases, diabetes in a child means a life sentence of twice-a-day shots, blood-sugar monitoring and constant concern about complications. I know many kids with this disease, and to me every last one of them is a hero. Sadly, we are diagnosing new cases of diabetes every month.

Most kids get type 1 diabetes formerly known as "juvenile onset." In this form, the body simply doesn't make enough of its own insulin. Without insulin, the body cannot take glucose from the bloodstream and transport it into the cells where it can be processed to fuel the body's energy needs. So insulin must be taken from a syringe.

What's frightening is that more and more "adult onset" or type 2 diabetes is showing up in younger people. This disease is primarily a result of obesity.[51] Fat decreases the response of cells to insulin. In other words, unlike type 1, the body produces enough insulin, but the receptors on cells are rendered unresponsive because of obesity. The cells read this as too little insulin. Glucose is not properly transported into the cells, remaining in the bloodstream where it eventually settles in the small blood vessels of the heart, kidneys, eyes, joints and brain, where it will only do harm.

The obvious and necessary treatment is weight control. Adults with type 2 diabetes can very often treat it successfully by simply losing weight. If done adequately, no insulin is required, and no long-term complications result.

This is an unnecessary problem for kids to face, especially since the cause—obesity—is preventable. The emergence of type 2 diabetes in the pediatric population is one problem that could be completely eradicated if obesity could be eliminated.

Orthopedic Problems: Doing the Heavy Lifting

Carrying around an overweight body all day is a tremendous strain on developing bones and joints—especially when that body is otherwise healthy and able to participate in sports, physical education and other vigorous activities involved in a normal, active, youthful lifestyle.

Located on the ends of normal bones in a growing child are the growth plates. These are soft, cartilage-like bones where new bone cells are being formed at a tremendous rate, making the bones grow longer.

The femur is that big bone of the upper leg, which fits into the hip joint. Occasionally, too much weight stress makes the growth plate of the femur slip, causing subtle knee or hip pain. Parents and teachers may notice that the child suddenly walks with a slight limp. This can become a serious problem if the "slipped" bone pieces compromise blood supply to the joint. Surgery is often required when that happens.[52]

For the first time in nearly twenty years of taking care of children, I recently saw a thirteen-year-old boy with a slipped disc in his lower back. This typically is a disorder of adulthood related to poor physical condition and improper weight distribution. He was a very nice kid who, according to his parents, had gained a lot of weight in the last couple of years. He was indeed quite fat, hated exercise and was as a result in poor physical condition. What he truly loved was riding and jumping show horses. After discussing this case with the neurologist, neurosurgeon, pediatrician and parents, we concluded that the stress of bouncing in the horse's saddle combined with his obesity put excessive strain on his weak lower back. Because his back was not strong enough to handle these stresses, he required surgery more commonly reserved for fifty-year-old men.

Although these are extreme examples, it is important to understand how obesity puts tremendous strain on bones and joints. Injuries can result that may affect a child for a lifetime. While it is important to participate in exercises essential to promoting healthy minds and bodies, kids cannot run, jump, bike or swim if there's too much fat in the way.

Psychological Effects: A Cross to Bear

We all have our crosses to bear. No one knows that more than a fat kid. And I know that best of all because I *was* a fat kid.

Perhaps this gives me empathy when dealing with over-weight children. However, the physical and psychological problems facing young people today are far more complex than anything I experienced as a child. This makes the stakes even higher for them and the pressures even greater.

One thing, however, is certain: The psychological and emotional trauma caused by childhood obesity is in many ways far more pervasive and dangerous than all of the purely physical effects combined.[53]

Depression is more common among children and teens than anyone realizes, and equally difficult to diagnose. If the root of a child's depression is his or her weight, then it is even more difficult to diagnose.[54] Obesity is a taboo in our culture, especially among children. If children are fat, parents have a very difficult time admitting it even to themselves. We make up all kinds of excuses. We rationalize, and we justify behaviors. But many times we just won't admit that the kids are fat.

This does them a great disservice. Even though we won't admit it, these kids are in pain. If they knew that parents recognized their pain and were willing to help, they would be so grateful and feel so much less alone.

It Begins with Shame

A friend of mine is a principal of a junior high school. She has told me many horror stories about the psychological trauma suffered by fat kids. One twelve-year-old boy wore sweaters to school every day well into the late spring when temperatures in Central Florida can be quite high. Teachers questioned him and peers teased him. Finally, the principal spoke to him in a nonthreatening manner. This boy was a chubby kid, and he was covering up his breasts that had become more pronounced as he gained weight.

He had not discussed this with anyone. Baring his soul to the principal helped, but imagine how much happier he could have been if he'd been able to deal with this horrible trauma at home.

What he was feeling was shame and humiliation, as if he had done something wrong. The breasts he was inappropriately developing were constant reminders to him that something he did or ate, or didn't do like exercise, was making him different from the other kids. His "deformity" was his punishment. Sadly, he felt he needed to be punished for being fat. And he was doing a very good job of it all by himself.

The Loss of Self-Esteem

When kids feel ashamed long enough, they lose their confidence. Why speak up in class if you are only going to get laughed at because of how you look? Why participate in sports if you are no good at any of them? Why talk to members of the opposite sex when you know they have no interest in talking to a fat kid? Live with these questions long enough and self-esteem goes right down the tubes.

Some kids overcompensate by seeking acceptance in other areas.[55] If you can't be popular because of the way you look or how you perform on the soccer field, perhaps you can get attention as the class clown, or imitating flatulence with your armpits. As you get older, kids might think you're cool if you skip a lot of classes, or get in trouble a lot with the principal, even if you are fat.

Why not be the bravest by trying drugs that the other kids are afraid to try? Why not "borrow" that hot car for a few minutes, just to take your friends for a joy ride? I know these sound like extreme examples, but they could all easily be true. Do not underestimate the loneliness that goes with being a fat kid, or the extent to which a left-out kid will go just to belong.

When Loneliness Leads to Despair

Children are motivated by wanting to belong, a manifestation of wanting to be loved. As kids mature, they transfer this need from their parents to their peers. To be loved by their friends, they must be like their friends, and therein lies the conundrum for fat kids.

You would think that because the number of fat kids is at an all-time high that there would be safety in numbers. Sadly, this isn't true. Fat kids are still in the minority. And the fatter they become the less they fit in.

By age six, children already begin to see fat people as different. According to one study, kids' perceptions of fat people are actually worse than their perceptions of those with disfiguring diseases.[56]

A boy I know gained a lot of weight between kindergarten and third grade. He was a smart, nice kid whom everybody liked. But as he gained weight, peers began to pick on him and fewer kids would play with him. Eventually he became miserably sad, and his schoolwork suffered. His parents mercifully transferred him to another school. After the first day, he was jubilant. He told his mother he was happy because he realized how nice it was that no one had picked on him that day.

I see quite a few teenagers in my practice who attempt suicide. I rarely get to know them well enough to see into the root cause of their despair, because I treat them only until they are medically stable. So I hear what you might expect: broke up with a boyfriend or girlfriend, hates parents, unwanted pregnancy, drug problems, problems with the law, and sometimes just plain depression. While obesity is never mentioned as a cause of attempted suicide, a great number of these kids are overweight.

Could the behavior that culminated in their suicide attempt have had its origins in obesity? Undoubtedly, there's no greater feeling of despair than feeling like an outsider . . . especially if you are an outsider because you're fat. But we will soon solve this deeply distressing problem, along with the many others, as you move on to "The Slim & Fit Program" (part II).

My goal in writing this section of *Slim & Fit Kids* is to give you a perspective on the epidemic of childhood obesity, tell my own story and lay the groundwork for the sections to follow: "Eating Slim & Fit"; "Thinking Slim & Fit"; and "Moving Slim & Fit." Soon you will have all the tools you need to deal with childhood obesity and help restore your child's health and self-esteem by enabling him or her to get slim and fit for a lifetime!

PART II

The Slim & Fit Program

Eight

Welcome to Slim & Fit Kids in Action

Call me the poster girl for skinny. As author of *The Beverly Hills Diet,* the diet phenomenon that sold over one million copies, I have been the nutritional guru to the likes of Jack Nicholson, Jodie Foster and Maria Shriver. Like other celebrities and jet-setters, they embraced my philosophy of Conscious Combining as the way to eat themselves skinny. For the last twenty years, I have maintained my own ideal weight of 102 pounds, navigating my way through the gourmet gauntlet of six world cruises and the dazzling Beverly Hills social scene.

But I wasn't always slim. In elementary school, I was the "two-by-four who couldn't get through the bathroom door." Though it happened more than forty years ago, I still remember the agony of enduring the yearly rite of passage in gym class when all the kids lined up at the scales to be weighed and measured. I kept maneuvering myself to the back of the line as the other kids stepped onto the scales while the teacher announced the results to the recorder. Finally it was my idol's, Patty Elder's, turn. "Seventy-five!" the teacher pronounced approvingly as Patty flounced prettily off the scales. Then it was show time. The room hushed as I stepped on, trying somehow to make myself small. "One hundred and nine!" the teacher pronounced in disbelief. The gym went wild, and I wanted to die.

I never wanted to be fat. No kid does. In fact, I started out life as a skinny, weighing in at birth at just five and a half pounds, the youngest skinny in a family of two other slender girls. I grew up a lithe little thing, always performing and mugging it up in family videos. Then at age nine, like John Monaco, ironically, I also underwent another rite of passage as predictable in the 1950s as puberty—a tonsillectomy. Etched in my mind is the first image I saw upon coming out of anesthesia. Looming over me, a spoon heaped with ice cream, was Mother. Was it then the seed was planted that food equals freedom from pain?

It was as if the "gene" that had kept me thin for the previous nine years had been removed along with my tonsils. Food that I'd eaten all my life suddenly was making me fat, just like what Dr. John Monaco experienced. Before I knew it, I'd become the fattest kid in my class.

If you were a fat kid or are the parent of one constantly struggling with his or her weight, you know what happened next. I compensated for my unfashionable size as any bright, articulate, "sensitive" outcast might do by forming clubs, electing myself as president, then starting the process all over again when the club had attracted enough members to vote me out. I became a secret eater, and my eating became the family obsession. "We can't eat delicatessen because Judy's on a diet," my mother would explain to my sisters. The same admonition applied to the rest of their favorite foods that they could eat without gaining an ounce. Now these were banned because they made me fat. This deprivation enforced on them by my fatness turned them sullen. My bedroom, separated by a long hall from the room they shared near my parents', was a constant physical reminder of my differentness. Being fat meant being friendless, alienated even from my own sisters. I turned for consolation to the only friends I had—food.

Before I'd graduated from grammar school, I'd become another overweight failure, huddled in the waiting room of fad-diet doctors, along with all the other miserable, fat and miserably fat kids from Chicago's north and south sides. Hooked on shots, thyroid pills, laxatives, appetite suppressants, pills, pills and more pills, I became a wired-up little kid with jangled nerves, constant headaches, insomnia and a waistline that wouldn't waste away. While all the other eighth graders shopped for frilly little graduation dresses in the children's department, I sulked along to Marshall Field's with Mom, desperately seeking an adult-sized dress suitable for a thirteen-year-old.

I didn't get slimmer and life didn't get easier in adolescence. High school and college were marked by the noticeable absence of boyfriends. On date-night Saturdays while other girls rocked at sock hops and made out with their boyfriends in the balcony at the Hamilton Theatre, I filled the void of loneliness with pizza binges, hiding the sad evidence in my neighbors' trash can.

Salvation finally arrived in my last year of college in the form of diuretics and the most potent diet pills I've ever taken, dispensed from Chicago's ultimate diet doctor. At five-feet, four-inches tall and pared down to 145 pounds, I was at long last "almost" thin (compared to my one-time high of 180), thin enough to leave my fat behind behind in Chicago. I decided to follow my heart and move to Los Angeles to study acting. After all, I'd prepared for an acting career all my life, first by pretending that being fat didn't hurt and later as a drama major to gain the self-confidence to carry off the pretense in front of other people. A slave to pills and near-starvation diets, I kept the weight down. But the toll on my psyche and my physical well-being was becoming perilously clear. Convinced that my lifelong battle with fat was caused not by what I ate but by some physiological malfunction, I entered the hospital for a battery of tests. Separated from the arsenal of pills that kept me souped-up and only semi-fat, my ten-day hospital stay netted a twenty-two-pound weight gain and an equally bleak verdict on the state of my health. My thyroid, adrenal and pituitary glands were shot. Half fat was as slim as I was going to get. I was given a life sentence—to maintain a semi-acceptable figure meant going through life half-drugged, dazed and totally disconsolate sustained on a staggering regimen of diet pills, diuretics and thyroid medications.

Then the answer almost literally slammed me in the face.

My first-ever skiing attempt landed me in the hospital with a broken leg. Without the distractions of dieting and diet pills, I experienced what was for me an epiphany. Being fat meant much more than being socially unacceptable. What it really meant was being unhealthy. With this new mindset, I devoured books on nutrition rather than nutrition-less junk food. I discovered that what's true for computers was also true for the human body—if you put garbage in (in terms of junk food), you get garbage out (in terms of a fat body). Fuel the body with the foods that energize it, and I could be fit, healthy, even perhaps slim.

Once my leg healed, I became a devotee of health-food stores, nutritionists and all of those who could demystify the relationship between food and health. In search of the Holy Grail of the perfect diet, I enrolled for six months as a student with the renowned nutritionist Scott Gershen. Grounded in both traditional medicine and the science of nutrition, he had a balanced, no-nonsense approach to eating that I trusted.

I was in search of the perfect diet, and my own body was my laboratory. A combination of circumstances culminating in my discovery of a book about enzymes and their effect on digestion resulted in the creation of my revolutionary new eating philosophy. Called Conscious Combining, it was based on the premise that enzymes play a decisive role in the digestion of food. How foods are eaten together is key to losing fat and maintaining weight. While the human body does require a balance of protein, carbohydrates and fat, balancing all of these requirements into a "square" meal is what undermines digestion. There are no "bad" foods—just bad combinations of foods. Improperly digested foods get "stuck" during the digestive process and wind up accumulating fat. But foods eaten in the right combinations pass through and out of the body so you don't gain weight.

Sound simple? It is. Because you can eat all the foods you love (as long as you eat them in the right combination), it's a snap to eat yourself skinny, fit and healthy. But don't just take my word for it, especially when it comes to my revolutionary way of thinking about how food can help your overweight child get slim and fit. Now John Monaco, M.D., a pediatric critical-care physician, endorses this diet. He knows firsthand the anguish fat children feel; he understands how obesity complicates and can even cause childhood illnesses to become life threatening. He's seen the desperation that demolishes young people's self-esteem, pushing those who feel most hopeless to suicide. Most importantly, he has the medical background to evaluate the science behind any diet. As my friend and coauthor, Dr. John has tried this diet himself, with his own young family and is now ready to share it with parents.

Together we have created *Slim & Fit Kids*. The program and the team we have put together represent a holistic approach to the entire complex of issues involved in dealing with an overweight child. Internationally acclaimed dancer and choreographer Thea White Riches, creator of the low-impact cardiovascular workout Jazz Funk and Sculpt 'N' Jam, has created Work It Out with Thea. Broken into short fifteen-minute segments, the program introduces kids to everything that's fun in getting slim and fit—kick-boxing, hip-hop and yoga, guaranteed to captivate even the least athletic kid. Michael Szymanski, certified personal trainer at the Pacific Athletic Club in Pacific Palisades, California, has created a program incorporating trigger-point massage and flexibility exercises for you to do with your youngster. Mariane Karou, creator of Dance Alive!, an innovative system of total physical movement synthesizing resistance training, isometrics and dance therapy, has developed a special program for your child to do at home. Christina Tsitrian and Francisco Cornejo-Mena, chefs extraordinaire, have created a whole new style of cuisine—Slim & Fit Pure Energy Gourmet Kid Cuisine—guaranteed to titillate the taste buds of even the tiniest tot.

With the help of these experts, we have put together a road map to help children regain self-esteem, develop a healthy body image, and fall in love with working out. *Slim & Fit Kids* will also help you rescue your family dynamics so that food no longer holds your household hostage. Through the guidance of family therapists Carol Yellin and Ellen Jones, we will help your "eater" and his or her siblings overcome their love/hate affair with food and fat. Overweight or obese children who hate themselves and are ostracized by classmates, who resent others in the family who seem to maintain their weight effortlessly, can plunge the entire family into a cycle of despair. What's the right way for a parent to respond when a child comes home crying because the kids at school called her fat and no one will play with her at recess? How do you help a teen rescue his psyche and his self-esteem when he's fat in a thin world? How can you prevent one child's weight problems from sabotaging the entire family's dynamics? These are some of the issues we will explore together in the "Slim & Fit Kids Program."

Childhood obesity can be treated. Not with a diet but with a vital new philosophy about how children can eat the foods they love while reclaiming their self-esteem, sculpting a new body and new body image. As parents, you can become their life support, their guide to becoming slim and fit (forever). In the process, you may even be tempted to apply the techniques we've developed to your own life.

Why not? What have you got to lose?

Nine

Ezra's Story

A Teenager Talks About His Struggles with His Weight and How the Slim & Fit Program Changed His Life

When it comes to being fat, and being the butt of kids' jokes, I've been there, done that. When I was in elementary school, I felt like I stuck out because I was always the chubbiest in my class. I tried to play Little League because my dad really wanted me to be on a team. But I wasn't really an efficient player. My weight made me slow, and I didn't feel like I had much energy. I just felt out of the loop so I quit after one season.

It was hard making friends because the kids were mean about my weight. What made matters even worse was the way other people often compared me to my older brother, Joe. One time we were at a family gathering when I was about nine. A relative looked at me and at Joe and said, "I don't understand how you can be brothers. You're so skinny, and he's so fat." I felt terrible.

My mother always told me I was handsome and not nearly as fat as I thought. She said she'd help me if I wanted to go on a diet and lose weight, but my heart wasn't really in it. I'd stick with something for a week, and then let it slide.

But when I got old enough to go to Cross Roads, one of the most prestigious high schools in L.A., things changed. It's really glamorous there and the kids are really into how they look. I began to feel that I was a real mess, inferior, and felt a lot of pressure to do something about my weight. I wanted to do something but didn't know what.

Then Judy Mazel appeared in my life. When Judy was developing the original *Beverly Hills Diet,* Mom and her friends had been on it and they were really close friends.

It was great to see Mom and Judy reunited. We decided she'd come over for dinner because Mom and Dad wanted to try the diet again after all these years.

What no one really knew was that I wanted to go on the diet as well. But I was embarrassed to tell Judy that I wanted to lose weight because I wanted to be good looking enough to compete with the other guys who weren't fat like me.

When Judy explained the basics of the *Slim & Fit Kids* program, it was so easy to follow. Everything was perfect about it except for the fact that I couldn't have fruit for dessert because you can't combine fruit with carbohydrates or protein. I loved the all-fruit days because everything tasted so good, and I felt really refreshed. A couple of times I developed a headache, so I did what Judy told me— listened to my body to figure out what I was craving. If it was protein, I waited two hours and then had some meat and the headache disappeared.

I'm also a sushi nut, and I had to change what I ate because most sushi has a lot of rice in it and one of the biggest rules on the diet is that you shouldn't combine protein with carbs. But it wasn't a big deal to work it out.

I dropped fifteen pounds. Then I plateaued for a couple of weeks. I felt like my body/mind were taking breaks together. I'd get lazy and forget to focus on combining foods properly, and my weight didn't move. Then I'd feel real motivated again and the weight would start to come off very fast again. I'd get so excited I'd weigh myself several times a day. Sometimes I lost two pounds a day. It was a terrific feeling, but I was also scared one day I'd wake up and find myself fat again.

But I haven't. Four months after I began Conscious Combining, I've dropped thirty-seven pounds. I have so much energy and feel just great about myself. It feels weird, like part of my body is disappearing. Now I look in the mirror and can see I'm not fat anymore, though I do still have some fat hanging around my belly and thighs. Now I want to lose another ten to fifteen pounds to really look cool.

Losing weight has motivated me to step up my exercise regime. In addition to yoga, which I've done for a long time, I added sit-ups. Suddenly I felt like my body wasn't working against me anymore, and I was capable of doing sit-ups. Now I can do two hundred at a time in sets of twenty. Even the yoga has become easier, and I can see a real difference in my personal performance.

So can the kids at school. Even the most popular kids—

especially the girls—have made it a point to let me know they notice the change and that they like what they've noticed. Not only have the most popular guys in the school found time to hang with me, but so has the most popular girl in my class.

I've always been a clotheshorse, but could never wear the stuff I've loved. Now I can actually fit into the clothes I've dreamed about. I asked Dad to take me to the Gucci store the other night. I just wanted to try on their jeans. My butt didn't stick out, and I looked really cool. I walked around the store in them, and I knew I could be anything I ever wanted to be thanks to *Slim & Fit Kids*.

**Ezra before
starting the program.**

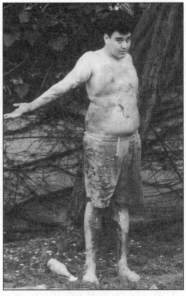

**Ezra after
losing fifteen pounds.**

**Ezra four months later—and
thirty-seven pounds lighter.**

SECTION I

Eating
Slim & Fit

Ten

Get Ready to Eat Slim & Fit

Now it's time to begin, time for you and your child to discover the keys to a new philosophy of eating that will change how you think about food forever. So take a last look at "fat" and let me welcome you to the world of Slim & Fit! The weight to be healthy and trim is over.

Why Kids Get Fat

In developing both *The Beverly Hills Diet* and *Slim & Fit Kids,* I never lost sight of the relationship between feelings and eating. Those of us who love to eat ("eaters") are a special category unto ourselves. The world has labeled us "sensitive." We're feelers who drown our hurts in food. Eating is the "Band-Aid" that somehow makes it possible for us to cope with disappointment, disapproval, rejection and fear. Of course, it also is our way of dealing with excitement; the highs, as well as the lows, when we have more on our plate figuratively than we can do, we soothe ourselves with food. Because "eaters" are high-energy, highly creative types, we're also geniuses at setting unrealistic goals. That means we're also constantly frustrated because our appetite for what we want to accomplish is often bigger than our ability, especially true for kids.

Then there is another type of child who also gets fat. I call them "products of society." They don't have an emotional attachment to their fat and to eating. They're the ones who have become obese because they ate too many foods with preservatives and chemicals, and drank too much milk. (You've already read what Dr. John says about the effect all those chemicals and milk have on our weight; suffice it to say, I second that motion.) These kids can easily lose weight and keep it off by tuning into their bodies and avoiding junk food, preservatives and chemicals. Unlike "eaters" who are perpetually on empty, these kids can actually act on the suggestion that they check in with their bodies to see if they're actually experiencing hunger before they go into the kitchen to eat. If they discover they're eating out of boredom or hurt feelings, they can actually stop. "Eaters" can't!

And that's why "eaters" particularly need the *Slim & Fit Kids* program: There are no portion controls, no time limits and no restricted foods. For an "eater," big portions are better; food feeds the soul as well as the body. I know all that because I'm still a compulsive eater. If I don't feel stuffed to bursting when I leave the table, I'm not happy. When someone tells me they stay thin by not eating after 6:00 P.M., my first question is, "What do you do for the rest of the night?" I'm not happy and likewise can't sleep if I don't eat something right before I'm ready to close my eyes. When I discovered the physical laws of digestion, enzymes and food combining, I was able to eat what I loved and *as much* as I loved and still get and stay slim. This is what I'm going to teach you and your child.

Modifying the Beverly Hills Diet for Kids

The original *Beverly Hills Diet* was very rigid. Carbohydrates were carbohydrates and went only with other carbohydrates. Likewise, protein was protein, and you only ate it with other protein. And never the two should meet. But as I began working with more clients and including children in the program, I began to see that it was possible to introduce more flexibility into the diet and still lose and maintain weight loss. In my new approach, which I first introduced in my book *The New Beverly Hills Diet,* dieters can mix foods occasionally, have proteins and carbohydrates together, so that when they have a hamburger with everything on it, they can also eat the bun, and the fries. Likewise, meat loaf and mashed potatoes don't have to be separate meals. As long as children start the day with an enzymatic fruit, they can get away with at least one miscombination (a protein and carbohydrate combination) a day. Kids who are fat because they're "products of society"—kids who leave food on their plates because their hearts are in their chests instead of their stomachs and what they put into their mouths—can probably get away with more. Of course, they won't be as healthy if they eat miscombinations because their digestive system won't work as efficiently. Those who stick the closest to the rules will feel the best and lose the most weight.

Following the rules to getting *slim and fit* is easy.

1. Begin each day with a fruit, preferably an enzymatic one (see the breakfast section of chapter 11).

2. Once your child has eaten something other than fruit, in other words once they've eaten something from another food group, they should not eat fruit again for the rest of the day. Remember, fruit digests almost instantly. If it is trapped in the stomach by other foods, it will not be absorbed or metabolized efficiently, and instead will rot and ferment, and cause extra pounds.

3. When your child moves on to eating carbohydrates, your child can also include soy products or any foods from my either/or list (see "Food Groups" at the end of this chapter).

4. Once your child starts eating animal protein, the balance of food he or she eats for the rest of day should consist mainly of protein. As Dr. John explained, when proteins and carbohydrates are combined, the body does not digest, absorb or metabolize the faster-digesting carbohydrates as they should because they are trapped in the stomach by the slower-digesting protein. Trapped food means maldigestion, and maldigestion equals fat. Also, as you may recall, the carbohydrate-digesting enzyme is annihilated by the presence of the protein-digesting enzyme.

5. Ideally, there should be a one-hour wait when switching from fruit to another category, and a two hour wait when switching from carbs and either/ors to animal protein.

6. Dinner is whatever the family is eating (even if it's miscombined!).

7. When mixing carbohydrates and proteins at the same meal . . . your basic, ahem, "balanced meal" . . . you can make it a more digestible combination for your child by ensuring that the protein portion is the bulk of the meal. This is for the same reason as rule four.

8. Avoid foods, oils and soft drinks with preservatives and chemicals. To do this, you must read the ingredients section on food labels carefully. (Teach your child to do the same.)

9. The ideal Slim & Fit day starts with fruit, moves on to carbs and either/ors, and ends however you or your child chooses.

Notice that I've taken the focus off dinner as the centerpiece of dieting. In today's hectic family life, dinner is a special catch-up time for the family to share their successes and disappointments. I don't want to make it the time when everyone focuses on what the "eater" is eating and how much weight he or she is gaining! Let your child eat whatever the family is eating. Yes, even if it's McDonald's or Kentucky Fried Chicken. Believe me, if your child eats fruit in the morning and basically follows the other rules, he or she will lose weight.

Welcome to the world of eating with joy where the joy of eating allows your child to enjoy losing weight!

How to Be Successful on the Program

In the pages that follow, you'll notice I've included lots of ideas on how to include soy, an either/or, in the diet. I'm not trying to turn everyone into vegetarians, but I am trying to help your children become slim and fit for a lifetime. Soy is a "super" food that can help them do just that! Because it contains all eight amino acids, it's a complete protein. It's low in fat, cholesterol free, and it also contains the B vitamins as well as being high in carbohydrates, fiber and calcium.

You'll also read about Blue-Green Algae in the "On Your Mark, Get Set . . ." section that follows. If your children ate nothing else but soy and Blue-Green Algae, their diet would probably be complete and their health off the charts!

If you're worried that your child is a finicky eater, you're not alone. Most children between the ages of four and ten are. Be patient and give it time. Try to keep in mind that your child is just asserting his or her sense of self, and hopefully your child will find our new Pure Energy Gourmet Kid Cuisine so enticing that his or her palate will prevail and feeding your child the Slim & Fit way will be a snap.

Lily Brumwell of Salt Lake City experienced major resistance from Sydnei, her five-year-old daughter. Lily found that she could overcome Sydnei's aversion to the texture of fruit by processing it first in the blender before serving. That was the first step. Now a child who wouldn't touch

fruit is enjoying it! Then Lily stopped force-
feeding Sydnei milk, which her daughter never even liked to begin with. Lily also stopped having cheese in the house by explaining that it simply wasn't healthy, not only that it was fattening. After

Lily Brumwell

Sydnei Brumwell

five years in the fat lane, Sydnei is finally becoming slim and fit.

If your child is like Sydnei and not the most cooperative, then go, as Lily did, a little more slowly. Begin by replacing the unhealthy snack items in your pantry with healthy equivalents (see the "Snacks and Nibbles" section of the next chapter). Keep reminding yourself that this is a process, not a race. Anything you do is better than doing nothing or continuing the bad habits that contributed to your child's current state. You are establishing lifelong lifestyle eating habits—and changing habits that are already formed, yours and your child's—so don't let your frustration at it "not happening instantly" stop it from happening at all. Don't give up or give in, and if all you can do is to convince your child to start each day with fruit, you'll be ahead of the gain, or rather game. Soon the pounds will begin to fall off, and the rest will follow.

By taking her toddler off preservatives and presenting fruit by itself instead of in combination with carbs and protein, Tara Rogachefsky of Miami, Florida, a follower of *The New Beverly Hills Diet*, stopped her son's projectile vomiting due

Tara and Ben Rogachefsky

to reflux syndrome. "Once I quit giving him crackers that contained preservatives, fast-food French fries cooked in oils containing chemicals, and restricted fruits to breakfast when they were eaten individually with no other foods, his vomiting stopped almost immediately. This way of eating also eliminated all the unpleasant symptoms connected with my irritable bowel syndrome. I'll never go off Judy's diet!"

For those of you who are familiar with the original *Beverly Hills Diet* or my *New Beverly Hills Diet,* you'll notice that the rules for kids are a lot more lenient than they are for adults. Kids can get away with a lot more. They don't have the years of physical, emotion and mental buildup that adults have. If you plan on making Slim & Fit eating a family affair, and you are doing it to lose weight yourself, I would suggest that you buy a copy of *The New Beverly Hills Diet* so that you can understand and incorporate the adult rules and mini-restrictions.

Although some recipes have been included, this is not a cookbook per se. Instead, what I've prepared for you is a guide that will teach you how to apply this revolutionary style of eating to what you already put on your plate at home, to the food your kids have known and grown to love, and how to fix these familiar foods and make them animal-protein free.

Trust me, by the time you've finished this book, you'll have learned everything you need to know about how to help your child be successful on this program.

On Your Mark, Get Set . . .

Here are a few last-minute instructions before your child takes that first bite:

1. The food group lists and other pertinent information follow this section. They are the foundation of this program. Refer to them a lot. Before you know it, you and your child will know them by heart, but until you do, use this book as a constant reminder.

2. Whatever you do that's better than what you're doing now is better than doing nothing. In fact, if all you get your child to do is eat or drink fruit in the morning, you're 50 percent ahead of the game. Don't expect to win the battle in one fell swoop. Remember, *you are dealing with a child*. If your child is being difficult about it, just go with it and don't push too hard. Your child will come around. Gradually start introducing Slim & Fit Gourmet Kid Cuisine in your child's lunch bag and start incorporating it into your evening meals. Between the recipes included in this book and those in my *New Beverly Hills Diet Recipes to Forever,* your child will soon see that eating Slim & Fit is not a punishment. Being able to eat French fries after school everyday is certainly not a prison sentence.

3. Kids either love or hate fruit. If you are lucky and your kids love it, you're home free. They will then probably love the "exotics," those specific tropical fruits high in enzymes: pineapple, papayas and mangoes. If, on the other hand, your child (like Sydnei) will maybe try one grape and spit it out, it's usually for one of two reasons: your child has a problem with the texture of the fruit or your child doesn't like the stickiness on his or her fingers. Many children can't stand that feeling. Smoothies and forks will remedy that. Fruit can be more than a finger food snack.

4. Salt—pass it as often as you can, or should I say pass *on* it. Most of those extra pounds your youngster is carrying is fluid trapped by all the salt in the fast foods he or she has been eating and the sodium base that's in all the chemicals preserving our food, compounding the effects of the maldigestion your child is experiencing from miscombining. Your child wasn't born with a taste for salt. In fact, children who spat out their baby food probably did so because it was too salty and they weren't used to it. Many snack foods come without salt added: tortilla chips, pretzels, crackers, popcorn and potato chips. They will say "no salt added" on the front of the package and are readily available in most supermarkets.

5. There are healthy equivalents for even the "unhealthiest" foods; reasonable, if not better-tasting, facsimiles of all these microwave delights that your kids have grown to love. Three brands to look for in the frozen food

section of your supermarket are Amy's Kitchen, Cascadian Farms and Cedarlane. From hot pockets to pizzas, they've covered all the bases, including how to package them *without using preservatives.* You'll also find the pricing competitive with most commercial brands.

6. Butter is fine. Please don't use margarine or imitation butter spreads.

7. No low-fat, no-fat or lite products that have chemical additives replacing the removed fat content.

8. No diet soda. Only the "real" thing, please. True, sugar isn't great, but it's a lot better than chemicals. . . . particularly aspartame, an ingredient found in most diet sodas, known to cause oxygen deprivation in the brain and convulsions at high altitudes. Your best choice would be some of the soft drink varieties available in health-food stores that use natural sweeteners. Check them out.

9. No artificial sweeteners. Again, even sugar would be better. Stevia, a very healthful herb available at health-food stores and the Slim & Fit Success Shop is an excellent natural sweetner and my first choice. Honey, molasses and maple syrup are also fine.

10. To fry or not to fry? Go ahead. It's just fine, but only use the oil once and make sure it is expeller pressed or unrefined. The label will state this. Safflower oil is best for deep-frying. The brands that you can trust and that are carried by most major supermarkets are

Hollywood, Hain and Spectrum. If you are using a breading, steer clear of the commercially packaged varieties that are loaded with salt, preservatives and MSG. Packaged tempura batter, however, generally has very few ingredients and most do not have a high sodium content or preservatives. *Again, read the labels.*

11. It is important that children are well hydrated and drink enough fluid, but you should only give children fruit juice in the morning before they have changed from fruit to another category. Remember the rule: Once they've switched from fruit to something else, do not go back to fruit that same day. If your kids have never tried vegetable juices, now is the time. Carrot juice is a real winner. Kids usually love it. Of course there is always tomato juice and V8. I would prefer, however, that you check out the choices of healthy fresh fruit and veggie juice now found in coolers at all major supermarkets. Water, of course, is best. Plain or sparkling seltzer only. The sparkling water with fruit essence is also fine, as it is only an essence. Avoid club soda as it is very salty. If your children are resistant because they haven't grown up drinking water, appeal to their logic. It's healthy for them or, if they're at "that age," it's also trendy.

12. To weigh or not to weigh? The scale—that little mechanical device has more effect on us than an atom bomb. I have seen the most powerful, most self-assured people shudder at the mere mention of

stepping on it. With my adults I show no mercy—daily weigh-ins are a must. The scale doesn't say good girl, bad girl. It represents reality. It reflects what we are and if what we are doing and eating works or doesn't work. With children, you have to tread gently so that they don't grow up with all the negative associations: the punishment of disapproval when they don't lose, the rewards when they do. Looking at the scale as a best friend, not a judge and jury, is important. If you treat their weigh-ins somewhat nonchalantly, that's what will happen. If they lose, just say, "Oh, isn't that terrific." No congratulations, and, please, *no rewards.* An "oh, great" is fine. If they haven't lost or if they have gained, don't issue any reprimands, accusations or give them the third degree. An audible "hmmm" is enough. Then go back to the drawing board. If you've been modifying the program a lot, try to follow it more closely. If you haven't stopped or cut back on salt, preservatives and dairy products, then perhaps now is the time. If you think your child is cheating, make available healthy equivalents of their favorite "cheat" foods (you'll find them in chapter 11, "Slim & Fit Pure Energy Gourmet Kid Cuisine"). *Emotion* is not allowed anywhere near the scale.

13. I have never been a proponent of dietary supplements, but there are a few that Dr. John and I consider important: *(1) Sesame seeds.* Sesame seeds are the richest natural digestible calcium source available

on the planet. All that concentrated calcium will not only be good for growing bones, it will also help your child sleep by relaxing the nervous system. Sesame seeds also provide extra fiber as well as lecithin and the three essential fatty acids you can acquire only from food. At bedtime, eat two heaping tablespoons of raw unhulled sesame seeds. Be sure they chew thoroughly. *(2) Vitamins.* A high-grade natural one-a-day multivitamin as well as a one-a-day multi-mineral supplement are good things to add to your children's daily plan. *(3) Cell Tech Blue-Green Algae.* Although similar products, such as Spirulina and Cholorella, as well as other brands of algae are available, *do not buy them.* I don't believe they compare to the nutritional wallop packed by Cell Tech Blue-Green Algae. Naturally harvested from a lake in Oregon and freeze-dried, I'm firmly convinced that these little seaweed tablets are so chock-full of natural nutrients that they could actually sustain life if more conventional food were not available. Unfortunately, this product is not available in retail stores, but I'll be happy to put you in touch with the source if you call the Slim & Fit Success Shop at 800-510-7973. For additional nutritional supplement recommendations, see your doctor.

14. The three most positive things that you can do to make the Slim & Fit program happen are to tell your child relax, have fun and find your family a health-food store and start using it.

Food Groups

Carbohydrates

Fruits (a carb in a category all its own)

All fruits—fresh and dried	Jam and jelly Fruit juice	Fruit nectar

Mini-Carbohydrates

Asparagus	Herbs	Mustard greens
Celery	Kale	Parsley
Crookneck squash	Lettuce	Spinach
	Mushrooms	Zucchini

Midi-Carbohydrates

Beets	Eggplant	Radishes
Broccoli	Leeks	Shallots
Brussels sprouts	Onions	String beans
Cabbage	Parsnips	Tomatoes
Carrots	Peas	Turnips
Cauliflower	Peppers (red, green and chili)	
Cucumbers		

Maxi-Carbohydrates

Artichokes	Cookies	Oats
Barley	Corn	Pasta
Breads	Cornmeal	Pie crust
Buckwheat	Couscous	Potatoes
Bulgur	Cream of Wheat	Rice
Cake (white, sponge, chocolate, carrot)	Farina	Rye
	Grains	Wheat
	Millet	Winter squash
Chocolate	Oatmeal	

50/50—Either/Or

Avocados	Lentils	Pinto beans
Garbanzo beans	Lima beans	Soybeans
Kidney beans	Peanuts	

Proteins

Beef	Milk	Desserts:
Cheese	Nuts	Cheesecake
Eggs	Nut butters	Crème brûlée
Fish	Pork	Crème caramel
Fowl	Seafood	Flan
Kefir	Seeds	Ice cream
Lamb	Yogurt	

Fats

Butter	Mayonnaise	Sour cream
Heavy cream	Oil	Whipped cream

Christina Tsitrian and Francisco Cornejo-Mena are the geniuses who've put the Slim & Fit Pure Energy Gourmet Kid Cuisine together. For more than twenty-five years, Christina has been involved with food and its relationship to self-esteem. Together they developed the Pure Energy Café concept that makes dining out as delicious as it is nutritious. Businessmen flock to the Café at the Pacific Athletic Club on their way to work, not necessarily to work out but to maximize their energy for the work ahead. Christina and Francisco have blended my technique and the Pure Energy concepts to provide accessible menus that are easy to prepare and provide a lifetime of health-conscious, tasty meals for kids of all ages.

The table is set, and now I turn it over to them. So draw up your chair and enjoy!

Bon appetit!

Slim & Fit

PURE ENERGY

Gourmet
Kid Cuisine

Eleven

Slim & Fit
Pure Energy
Gourmet
Kid Cuisine

Christina Tsitrian   **Francisco Cornejo-Mena**

This chapter is a guide to getting the most flavor and nutrition as well as having the most fun with your new way of eating.

Our goal is to stimulate your mind and appetite with enough ideas to present the Slim & Fit Pure Energy Gourmet Kid Cuisine as a mouthwatering adventure to achieve your child's goal weight and a lifetime of healthful enjoyment of your food. Together with the recipes and suggestions we've included here, our follow-up cookbooks and Judy Mazel's *New Beverly Hills Diet Recipes to Forever,* your support system is in place—so go for it! The way your child eats will make the difference you both desire.

Ingredients

First and foremost, always start with the freshest ingredients possible. It makes a difference in flavor. In general, we have found the produce section of most markets have personnel on duty to guide you to the best of what's available, as well as how to store produce with which you are unfamiliar. We suggest you pick up a copy of *The New Beverly Hills Diet Little Skinny Companion* for a detailed description of how to select ripe fruit.

Stock your pantry with items that have been processed without additives and preservatives. Choose brands of oil that are unrefined or expeller-pressed safflower oil for high-heat cooking, virgin olive oil and sesame oil for dressings and sauces. Have on hand a variety of dried herbs and commercially prepared sauces with no hydrogenated oils, dairy products or animal protein, and a minimum of salt, if any. Choose breads that have no dough conditioners.

Remember, heat and light have a degenerative effect on all foods. Organize storage in your pantry away from the heat of the stove and direct sunlight. Foods such as garlic, onions, potatoes, yams and most root vegetables should be stored in a cool, dry, dark place. Fresh produce should be stored after any tattered or bruised parts have been removed. Wrapping them lightly in paper towels will reduce the growth of bacteria naturally occurring in food with a high-moisture content.

A flavorful kitchen is a fun kitchen. Your child's diet should provide flavors that you both enjoy. When planning your dieter's menu, start with a list of foods that your child enjoys. Most of them will fall into certain categories of either preparation or ethnic cuisine. With a few seasoning mixes and simple cooking techniques, you can create meals for your children that will answer the desires of their palates without compromising their goal to achieve a body that is well balanced in terms of nutrition and weight.

Cooking Techniques

The techniques that follow are basic and should get you through most any recipe you encounter. We recommend that you equip your kitchen with labor-saving devices such as a food processor, a blender, a steamer, electric or stove-top griddle, and, of course, a good set of knives. You will also need a cutting board, storage containers and a set of mixing bowls. Most culinary supply stores will be happy to guide you to the basic items a working kitchen needs. In our follow-up cookbook, we will elaborate on this list.

Grilling can be done on a stovetop with a griddle pan, on a griddle or on a barbecue. Items you are going to grill should have a light coating of oil and should be marinated in the seasoning of your choice for at least 5 minutes. It is best to lightly pierce the surface of the food all over before marinating. The heat source should be a medium-high to high heat before cooking begins. Except for poultry, a good rule of thumb is to cook each side about 3 to 4 minutes.

Steaming is done by placing food in a covered strainer-type basket and suspending the basket above a small amount of boiling water. Steaming should only take a few minutes. Be careful not to oversteam as food will become soft and mushy, and remember to keep your pot covered throughout the process.

Roasting is done in the oven. Food should have a light coating of oil. If you keep some olive oil or safflower oil in a spray bottle, it makes this very easy. Put food in one layer on a roasting pan. Do not overcrowd. You should preheat the oven to 475°F for quick roasting or 275°F for slow roasting.

Baking is done in the oven at a medium heat. The oven should be preheated between 325°F and 375°F. The process usually involves 45 minutes to 1½ hours.

Broiling uses a heat source that is above the food and is generally at a very high heat. Food cooks quickly and you should not leave it unattended. The rule is 3 to 4 minutes on each side.

Boiling is done on top of the stove. It requires a pot about three times larger than the amount of food you will be cooking. The water level can vary with recipes, but in general you should cover the food by at least three inches of water, and the water should be at the boiling point before the food is put into it.

Sautéing is done on top of the stove. A frying pan and a little oil brought to a medium-high heat gets you started. Your food items should be sliced or chopped to about a ½-inch to 1-inch width. Do not overcrowd. Your goal is to get a nicely browned color on all sides. This will take a few minutes per side. Do not overstir. It can cause mushiness.

Pureeing is a method of breaking down food to a smooth consistency. You can puree food with a ricer, a strainer, a blender or a food processor. For ease, we recommend you use a blender or immersion blender, or the food processor.

Chopping is when food is cut into relatively large pieces. A large chop is food cut into about 1½-inch to 3-inch pieces. A small chop is food cut into about ½-inch to 1-inch pieces.

Dicing means cutting food into about ½-inch cubes. Small dice means to cut food into about ¼-inch cubes.

Mincing means dicing food into about half the size of a small dice, or ⅛-inch cubes.

Slicing usually means cutting food from top to bottom in ½-inch widths.

Flavoring Agents and Seasoning Mixes

Flavoring agents and seasoning mixes are what lend character to the foods we prepare. When purchasing these items, do not buy large quantities, as their shelf life is six months to a year, and that is only if they are stored properly. After that period, their flavor potency may decrease dramatically. Stock your cupboard with: safflower oil, olive oil, sesame oil, toasted sesame oil, low-sodium tamari, rice vinegar, Bragg Liquid Aminos and no- or low-sodium vegetable broth (available through our Slim & Fit Success Shop [800-510-7973] or at health-food stores). Keep a variety of dried herbs on hand, including: rosemary, oregano, dill, basil, parsley, fennel, marjoram, thyme, mint and lemongrass. If you use fresh herbs, add them to the dish at the end of the cooking process.

You can purchase spices individually or premixed. You should have the following in your cupboard: curry, chili powder, gomasi (health-food store or Slim & Fit Success Shop), grilling spices, cajun spice mix, cinnamon, nutmeg, cloves, star anise, Mrs. Dash salt substitute, black pepper, allspice, cumin, cardamom, ground coriander seeds and cayenne. If you want to turn a dish into something special, you can also add dehydrated garlic and onion, vegetable flakes, sun-dried tomatoes and bell pepper flakes.

Seasoning mixes will shorten your time in the kitchen and will help add a carefree flow to your kitchen preparation. We group our mixes in ethnic categories. The following recipes will yield about a half-cup, which is enough to flavor several different dishes.

Greek Mix

8 tablespoons Greek oregano	*1 tablespoon garlic powder*
2 tablespoons rosemary	*1 tablespoon onion powder*
3 tablespoons thyme	*1 tablespoon black pepper*
3 tablespoons parsley	*½ teaspoon nutmeg*

Southwest Mix

8 tablespoons ground cumin
5 tablespoons chili powder
½ teaspoon nutmeg
2 tablespoons garlic powder
2 tablespoons onion powder

8 tablespoons bell pepper
   flakes
4 tablespoons oregano
4 tablespoons paprika

Italian Mix

8 tablespoons oregano
3 tablespoons thyme
2 tablespoons marjoram
3 tablespoons basil
¼ teaspoon crushed red
   pepper

1 tablespoon garlic powder
1 tablespoon onion powder
2 teaspoons rosemary
1 tablespoon fennel

Asian Mix

6 tablespoons cumin
1 tablespoon garlic powder
1 tablespoon onion powder

1 tablespoon coriander
1 teaspoon nutmeg

Menu Preparation

Preparation is the key to the outcome of all your culinary efforts. Yes, culinary efforts. Anytime you prepare something someone is going to eat or drink, you are in the culinary realm. It can be as simple as squeezing a lemon in a glass of water or as complex as preparing a seven-course meal! It's all about attitude. If your mouth is watering for a bagel and cream cheese there can be a world of difference in the quality of the bagel or the quality of the cream cheese. There is a certain characteristic of every appetite desire that can span a lifetime of experiences. Our feeling is that if you get the basics, you can experiment to achieve yours and your child's hearts' desires.

Ideally, you are in the frame of mind that you and your child are in control of his or her well-being. The subject of food should have a good effect on your child. Your child's mouth should water at the prospect of the next mouthful. This can become a lifetime experience once your child adjusts to the fact that eating should not be an in-between process among everything else in daily life. In order for you and your child to have control of meals (*especially* if this involves new foods), you as the cook need to plan ahead. This simplifies the process. The following are some tips on preparing and having the basic ingredients of your child's meals. We are by no means the final word. The world of delicious food is common to many people. Your local bookseller has numerous cookbooks that represent flavors from all over the world and chefs who share their culinary adventures and experience. You can incorporate almost any flavor into a healthy recipe. You will find this to be a daily adventure on the path to a gratified palate and a well-balanced weight for your youngster.

The beginning of the week is a good time to make some staples ahead of time. Cook pastas, rice, soups, pestos, loaves and casseroles in batches. For example, if preparing rice for two, make enough for three or more meals. If you are baking, put some russet potatoes or yams in the oven, and maybe throw in a winter squash along with whatever else is in the oven. This will give you a base for another meal. This type of preparation is a perfect example of how planning ahead can simplify meal preparation. These items store well in your refrigerator or freezer. Have meal-sized storage containers on hand. It will save time, and the food will stay fresher. Rice and pasta store well in a Ziplock-type plastic bag, as do most foods that aren't too juicy.

You can cook vegetables ahead of time. Steaming, grilling, roasting and marinating can be done one to two days ahead. Frozen vegetables can be on hand, but we don't recommend them for grilling or roasting.

Pestos and sauces are usually good for up to a week if kept in your refrigerator. These should never be left sitting out. Take what you will use and immediately return the rest to the refrigerator. Airborne bacteria will affect the freshness, quality and flavor.

You can make beans and legumes ahead of time and store them in the refrigerator or freezer. Remember, in all cases, storing meal-sized containers is best for freshness. In our experience, these foods are more perishable than other foods, so please note if you freeze them, they will tend toward a soft texture. In the refrigerator, they will hold up better with a light coat of oil.

For BBQ, smoky or Oriental flavor, try toasted sesame oil. A little dash will do you, so use a light hand. You'll find it in the Asian food section of your market. Also, the leafy-green lettuce-like vegetable arugula has a nice smoky flavor that goes great in salads and chilis. Arugula is best used at the end of the cooking process, uncooked.

The Joy of Soy

One of the ways to ensure that Pure Energy eating will become a way of life for you is to familiarize yourself with and begin to use soy and the wide range of products available. As Judy said earlier, if we only had soy and Blue-Green Algae as food sources, we could probably live a very healthy life and lack nothing nutritionally. Soy is easy to use and far more economical than animal protein, and is an easy-to-digest protein alternative with a plethora of health benefits as Dr. John pointed out in chapter 4.

Containing all nine essential amino acids, soy is recognized as a complete protein and can easily replace animal protein in one's diet.

And moms . . . a little aside: In an article I read recently in *Women on the Move* by journalist and movement artist Anita De Francesco, she states that:

> *The soybean is also one of the best sources of estrogen. It has proved effective in reducing menopausal discomforts, especially hot flashes. The estrogen genistein attaches to cell receptors and has been successful in hindering the*

growth of cancer cells, thereby prevent-ing certain types of breast cancers.

In Japan, soy is a regular part of the daily diet. Recent studies prove Japanese women have far fewer reported cases of breast cancer than do American

Anita De Francesco *women. Doctors attribute this to the high soy diet of Japanese women. Soy may be the ultimate food of the millennium.*

Textured Soy Protein (TSP)

Textured soy protein, often called TSP or TVP, is made from de-fatted soy flour that is compressed and processed into granules or chunks. It is sold as a dried, granular prod-uct. When it is rehydrated with boiling water, TSP has a tex-ture similar to ground beef. It's also available in chunk-size pieces that can replace stew meat in any recipe. Having no flavor of its own, TSP will take on any flavor you desire with the proper seasonings. We recently served some BBQ pork lo mein made with TSP to a vegetarian friend. It tasted so like the "real" thing that she almost refused to eat it. Use TSP in your favorite meat loaf recipe and no one will even know the difference. It is best when soaked overnight.

Tofu

Tofu, also know as soybean curd, is a soft, cheese-like food made by curdling hot soymilk with a coagulant. Tofu, like TSP, acts like a sponge, soaking up whatever flavors you add to it. Crumble it in a pot of chili sauce, and it tastes like chili. Blend it with cocoa or carob and sweetener, and it becomes a double for chocolate-cream pie filling. There are three main types of tofu: firm, soft and silken. Firm tofu is dense and solid. It holds up well in stir-fry dishes, soups or on the grill. We even like it plain, sliced and quickly fried in hot oil, then dipped in almost any kind of a sauce, particularly hot-chili toasted sesame oil. Soft tofu is good for recipes that call for blended tofu. Silken tofu is creamy and easily replaces cream cheese or ricotta cheese in a recipe. It is also great for dips. For sandwich slices, pour off the liquid, cut the tofu into thick slices, coat it with one of your favorite sauces and bake it for about 30 minutes at 350°F.

Edamamé

Edamamé are large soybeans harvested while the beans are still green. They are not only a great side-dish vegetable; they are also a super snack food.

Tempeh

Tempeh is a chunky, tender soybean cake made from whole soybeans and another grain, such as rice or millet. It has a smoky, rather nutty flavor. Marinated and grilled, it's a great addition to soups, casseroles or chili.

Other Soy Products

The list of other soy-derived, prepared products is long and varied: soy-based infant formula; soy yogurt; soy milk; nondairy frozen dessert (as good as ice cream); soy cheese; soy flour; tamari and soy sauce; soy sprouts. You'll find soy equivalents for everything from hot dogs, bologna, turkey breast, pastrami and ready-to-use "hamburger meat," to puddings, desserts and even whole-meal frozen dinners.

A word of caution: Don't have unrealistic expectations when it comes to taste. If the pastrami doesn't taste exactly the same as the pastrami you get at the Stage Deli in New York, that doesn't make it bad, just different. A baked potato might taste better with salt, but it's still darn terrific without salt. Enjoy all foods for what they are, and the negative side effects of the "unhealthy" equivalents won't enjoin you.

"The Soyfoods Directory" is a wonderful booklet that will tell you just about everything you need to know about soy, including where you can find the different products in your supermarket. You can obtain it by calling 800-TALKSOY.

Following are some simple methods of helping your child achieve his or her mealtime goals. We will begin with the first meal of the day, move on to snacks, and culminate with lunch. You will find that oftentimes our recipes will serve your child through the dinner meal as well.

Breakfast

Fruit, remember, starts the day. It can be breakfast in the form of a smoothie, a fruit salad, or just a big bowl of a single fruit. Don't stint on the portions. Make sure your child is really full—the more fruit she eats the better. After breakfast, send your child off to school with some dried fruit, a bag of cereal or a bagel for the next time he or she is hungry. The fruits most recommended for that morning start, those high in natural enzymes and nutritionally superior, are:

pineapple	kiwi
papaya	mango
grapes	persimmon
watermelon	cherries
blueberries	dried apricots*
raspberries	dried prunes*
blackberries	raisins*
strawberries	figs—dried* or fresh

Fruits obvious in their absence include apples, oranges, and grapefruits. This familiar trio we've all known and loved growing up do not make great day starters. They just don't fill kids up, and what you don't want is to have your child getting hungry and feeling deprived a half hour after she's eaten.

---

*Avoid dried fruits with sulfur dioxide or potassium sorbate.

Smoothies

In general, smoothies are blended drinks that serve as either meals or in-between-meal snacks, depending on the recipe. Smoothies require a blender, a recipe that includes fluid (usually a juice) and about one cup of a fruit or similar food. If using frozen fruit, no ice is needed. However, if using fresh ingredients, you will have to add about three-quarters of a cup of ice. When preparing smoothies, first put the juice in the blender, then the fruit, and finally any other additives. Start your blender at low and move up to puree mode. You will need to run your blender for 2 to 3 minutes to complete the smoothie.

Tropical Frost

1 frozen banana   ½ cup pineapple
½ cup orange juice

Peach Blossom

½ cup peaches   1 frozen banana
1 cup apple juice

Blueberry Lust

1 cup frozen blueberries*   ½ cup pineapple juice
1 fresh banana

Strawberry Rush

1 cup strawberries   ½ cup apple juice
1 frozen banana

Mango Madness

2 frozen bananas   1 cup frozen strawberries*
2 mangoes, sliced   apple juice to desired
1 cup frozen blueberries*   smoothness and thickness

---

*Fresh can be substituted for frozen, but remember to add the ice.

Fruit Salads

Pure Energy Ambrosia

½ cup pineapple
½ cup grapes
½ cup grated apple

dash of cinnamon
squeeze of lemon

Strawberry Mint

1 cup strawberries
squeeze of lemon
4 mint leaves chopped

sprinkle of sugar or a
drop of stevia

Berry Banana

1 cup berries
1 sliced banana

¼ cup dried bananas
toss with a little juice

Berry Truly Yours

1 cup strawberries   1 banana, sliced
1 cup blueberries

Peach Keen

1 cup apricots   1 cup blueberries
1 cup peaches

Tropical Treat

1 cup mango   1 cup pineapple
1 cup papaya   1 banana, sliced

Snacks and Nibbles

Somewhere between breakfast and lunch, little bodies—
even big little bodies—need a little fortifying. Carbohydrate
snacks are good any time throughout the day until animal
protein is consumed. Remember: once your child consumes
animal protein, stick only to the protein snacks. See rule
four at the beginning of chapter 10 if you have any
questions.

Carbohydrate Snacks (salt-free is best)

potato chips	rice cakes
pretzels	bread of any kind (without
tortilla chips	dough conditioners, please)
popcorn	crackers
peanuts	roasted soy nuts or other soy
yam chips	products (watch the salt)
vegetable sticks	French fries
peanut butter	onion rings

Protein Snacks

nuts and seeds of any kind, preferably raw and unsalted	roasted soy nuts
	ice cream (preferably soy)
nut butters, including peanut butter	yogurt (preferably soy)
	cheese (preferably soy)

Lunch

Tacos

Tacos are a versatile dish that you can make with the following fillings or use your imagination and make up your
own. For soft tortillas, warm each side for 30 seconds in a
nonstick fry pan or on a griddle at 375°F. For hard-shell
tacos, quickly deep-fry in unrefined safflower oil until
golden.

1. Ortega chilies, sautéed onion, cabbage, cilantro, garlic
   and jalapeño pepper (soycheese optional), TSP or tofu

2. Roasted potatoes and salsa

3. Grilled eggplant, zucchini, roasted red peppers, grated
   soy cheese, avocado and chopped green onions

4. Black beans, portobello mushrooms, radish sprouts
   and salsa (soycheese optional)

Wraps and Burritos

These are basically the same when it comes to preparation. Begin by warming the tortillas on the stovetop. This
takes about a minute or less. Lay the tortilla out flat. Place
the filling about three inches away from the edge closest to
you, leaving a 1- to 2-inch border on the sides. Lift the edge
closest to you over the filling. Bring the side edges over the
filling to meet the first fold, similar to an envelope fold. With
both hands, roll it forward, using your fingers to tuck the

filling into the tortilla firmly. Continue rolling until you reach the end of the tortilla. Trust us, you'll know when you are done. At this point you can either serve as is or cut into two to four pieces.

Burritos

Burritos are designed to be a complete meal. We recommend adding sprouts or shredded lettuce to any and all of them. When making a burrito, be sure your fillings are not too juicy; the moisture will disintegrate the tortilla. Here are a few suggestions, or let your imagination run wild:

1. Red beans and rice, with roasted tomato salsa and soy cheese

2. Textured soy protein, chilies, guacamole, Spanish brown rice, roasted fresh corn, cilantro and chopped onion

3. Grilled vegetable, brown rice, Italian dressing and fresh basil

4. Sliced BBQ-style tempeh, crushed peanuts, brown rice, bean sprouts and Thai-style dressing

Wraps

Wraps are easy to tote and easy to make. Whatever your dream lunch, you can wrap it up! We recommend leaving them whole if it's a meal on the run. We particularly like to wrap salad versions of our favorite foods. It's easy, you just chop your ingredients, put them in a bowl, mix them with a sauce, wrap them up, and you've got a yummy meal! Once again, don't stop here. Think of some of your child's favorite foods and just wrap them up to go.

1. Caesar salad with tempeh and French green beans

2. Mock egg salad, bean sprouts, arugula, brown rice, celery, cabbage and peppers

3. Southwest-flavored tofu, guacamole, salsa, black beans, cilantro, roasted pepper pesto, and shredded lettuce or sprouts

4. Grilled tofu with savory spices, grilled onions, peppers and cucumber-garlic sauce

Pizza

Pizza is a comfort food, and we think we could live on it alone. This is also a versatile dish. We like to use tortillas or a pre-made, store-bought crust for a quick method. Carefully read the labels and avoid any crusts with dough conditioners, and other chemicals or preservatives. With tortillas, you can prepare pizzas on the stovetop in just a few minutes. We basically start with sun-dried tomato pesto (see the recipe included in the "Pesto" section) or a simple marinara, and add our toppings according to what's on hand or what we're in the mood for.

1. Roasted peppers, garlic, fresh basil and tofurella

2. Greek olives, mushrooms and capers

3. Garlic and capers

4. Fennel, eggplant, zucchini, garlic, thyme and basil

5. Italian-flavored textured soy protein, peppers, mushrooms and basil

6. Tomato sauce and soy cheese

Pasta

To keep it an all-carbohydrate dish, if you want to sprinkle on some Parmesan cheese use the rice parmesan (made from rice) instead of regular.

1. Spaghetti with tomato sauce

2. Noodles with butter

3. Penne with vegetables

4. Macaroni and cheese (soy cheese, of course)

Quesadillas

Quesadillas are toasted cheese sandwiches made with tortillas instead of bread. They are a lot of fun, and they're quick. With as little as three ingredients and not many more minutes, your child can have a tasty treat or a simple meal. We love these so much we always have some soy cheese and tortillas in the fridge.

1. Artichoke and corn with Ortega peppers

2. Avocado and salsa

3. Salsa and soycheese

4. Braised cabbage, green onions and cilantro

5. Grilled mushrooms, arugula and sautéed onion

6. American-style soy cheese, mustard, pickles and grilled onions

7. Marinated grilled eggplant and garlic with fresh basil

8. Roasted peppers and cilantro

Sandwiches

Sandwiches are an all-time favorite. Your child is not restricted to whole-grain bread. Any bread is fine—even white bread, as long as it does not have preservatives or dough conditioners. If you are serving your child a whole-grain bread, you'll find toasting it adds a nice, nutty flavor kids love.

1. All-American-style garden burger, grilled onions, pickles, mustard and cheddar-style soy cheese

2. Mock egg salad, lettuce, tomato and red onion

3. Veggie loaf made with roasted peppers, onions, textured soy protein and mushrooms; spread with pesto and top with sprouts

4. Grilled veggies with sun-dried tomato pesto

5. Grilled tofu with arugula and roasted peppers

6. Roasted tomatoes, onions, tofu and mushrooms

7. Cucumber, cilantro, tomato, red onion and pepper jack cheese

8. Avocado, sprouts, tomato, red onion and eggplant pesto

9. Peanut butter

10. Avocado, tomato and sprouts

11. Lettuce, tomato, onion, cucumber

12. Soy lunchmeats

Soup

Soup is the staff of life as far as we're concerned. You can make soup out of almost anything and eat it anywhere and anytime. Soups can be hot or cold. A good soup thermos is a must. You can adapt any of your child's already-favorite veggie-oriented soups to Slim & Fit by using low- or no-sodium vegetable broth instead of beef or chicken, and soy milk instead of cow's milk.

1. Garden vegetable

2. Mushroom and barley

3. Potato and corn with Ortega peppers

4. Butternut squash

5. Carrot with rosemary and orange zest

6. Chunky vegetable and lentil

7. Split pea with fennel and roasted peppers

8. Tortilla and roasted corn

9. Fresh tomato and basil

10. Gazpacho

11. Cucumber and yogurt

12. Yam and squash

13. Chili

14. Mediterranean white bean soup

15. Curry with tofu

16. Spring vegetable soup with fragrant herbs and grated veggies

17. Orzo with tomatoes and onions

Vegetables

Vegetables, which are carbohydrates, are the amazing stars of all the food groups. They lend color, texture, flavor and wholesomeness to our diets. They have fiber and are nutrient rich. They have the most versatility of all foods in terms of their preparations. They can be stored in a variety of ways and still maintain their quality.

When grilling vegetables, most vegetables need to be cut to about ½-inch thicknesses. They can be cut from top to bottom or straight across. Preheat your heat source. This takes about 5 to 10 minutes, depending on what kind of heating element you are using. If you have to wait a few minutes, you can take this opportunity to marinate your vegetables. Once your heat source is preheated, place your veggies right on or in the grill or griddle, in the oven or under the broiler.

Peruse any of the cookbooks you have on hand, and you'll see that there is no end to what you can do with vegetables, including tempura, stir-fried or curried. These are just a few ideas. We're sure you'll have some of your own.

1. Steamed broccoli with olive oil and garlic

2. Sautéed spinach with basil, garlic and nutmeg

3. Green beans with toasted sesame oil

4. Fresh corn with tarragon and tomatoes

5. Asparagus with roasted pepper pesto

6. Summer squash with rice parmesan and olive oil

7. Carrots with fresh mint and brown sugar

8. Grilled zucchini, eggplant, red onion and mushrooms in Italian dressing

Casseroles and Loaves

These require a baking dish. You will need one of the following depending on the recipe: a casserole dish, a loaf pan or a baking pan. You will need to sparingly coat the pan with safflower oil. Remember to preheat your oven.

Casserole and loaf-style meals are very handy to prepare ahead of time. You can make large quantities, then divide the casserole into individual portions and freeze them for future use. A casserole can be served as a one-dish meal, as a main course with a side dish, or as a side dish itself. They are a great way to use up leftovers. Some casseroles can be served hot or cold. We often thinly slice these and use them as appetizers.

1. Lentil loaf made with roasted peppers and mushrooms

2. Garbanzo bean and sweet onion loaf with Middle Eastern spices

3. Broccoli with ground soy nuts and cheddar-style soy cheese

4. BBQ tofu, brown rice and green bean loaf

5. Macaroni and cheddar-style soy cheese bake

6. Tamale pie with rice parmesan, peppers and corn

Rich and Hearty Veggie Loaf

¼ cup olive oil
1 cup chopped onions
1 cup chopped portobello
  mushrooms
2 medium carrots, grated
⅓ can tomato paste
1½ cups textured soy protein

1 tablespoon minced garlic
2 teaspoons dried thyme
1½ teaspoons toasted sesame oil
1 tablespoon mustard of your
  choice
Mrs. Dash salt substitute and
  pepper to taste

Preheat oven to 375°F. Lightly coat a loaf pan with olive oil. Set aside. Heat oil in a large skillet on medium-high heat until the oil start to sizzle. Add onions, mushrooms, carrots and tomato paste. Stir to coat all the veggies. Add the remaining ingredients and sauté for 5 to 7 minutes, stirring occasionally. Remove from heat and let cool for a few minutes in a large bowl. Bring mixture together in a ball shape with your hands. Place in loaf pan, pressing firmly to the form of a loaf. Bake for 30 to 45 minutes until firm to the touch and slightly brown on top. Remove from the oven and let cool 10 minutes before slicing.

Tamale Pie

2 tablespoons olive oil
1 cup chopped onions
2 tablespoons cumin
2 tablespoons chili powder
1 tablespoon dried oregano
1 tablespoon minced garlic
1 teaspoon toasted sesame oil
1 cup chunky-style salsa
1 cup chunky-style roasted
   pepper salsa

1 bunch fresh cilantro,
   chopped
4 sliced green onions
1 small package frozen
   spinach, drained and
   chopped
½ cup rice Parmesan
1 package firm tofu crumbled
1 package thin corn tortillas
2 cups jalapeño pepper soy cheese

Preheat oven to 375°F. Lightly oil a medium-sized casserole dish or baking pan. Heat oil in a large skillet until it sizzles. Add onions, cumin, chili powder, oregano and garlic. Sauté for a few minutes. Transfer to a large mixing bowl. Add remaining ingredients, except for soy cheese and tortillas. Spread a small amount of the mixture on the bottom of the dish in a thin layer. Place tortillas in one layer to cover the bottom of the dish, overlapping or spreading them out to fit. Alternate layers of vegetable mixture and tortillas, ending in a final layer of the mixture. Sprinkle soy cheese on top. Bake for 30 to 45 minutes until firm to the touch and slightly brown on top. Remove from oven and let cool for a few minutes before serving. Serve as is or with salsa on the side. This dish goes well with a salad or veggies as side dishes.

Harvest Vegetable Soup

2 tablespoons olive oil or
  vegetable oil
1 onion, chopped
4 ribs of celery, chopped
2 large carrots, chopped
1 rutabaga, chopped coarsely
1 turnip, chopped coarsely
2 tomatoes, chopped
4 large mushrooms, chopped
1 red bell pepper, chopped

1 green bell pepper, chopped
1 zucchini, chopped
1 yam, peeled and grated
1 bunch Italian parsley,
  chopped
1 bunch basil, chopped

1 quart of vegetable broth or
  water
½ can tomato paste
2 tablespoons oregano
1 tablespoon thyme
2 tablespoons chopped garlic

1 tablespoon hot sauce
3 or 4 teaspoons Worcestershire
  sauce
2 teaspoons Mrs. Dash salt
  substitute
1 teaspoon black pepper

Warm oil in a large stockpot or Dutch oven. Add onion, celery, carrots, rutabaga, turnip, tomatoes, mushrooms, and peppers, and sauté, stirring occasionally. Meanwhile, chop zucchini, grate yam, and chop parsley and basil. By the time you are finished, the vegetables will be sautéed. Add broth or water and tomato paste. This should cover the mixture with two inches of fluid. A little more or less won't matter. Add remaining ingredients and cook until vegetables are fork tender, about 20 to 30 minutes. Taste and adjust salt and pepper as needed.

Pesto

When it comes to pesto, a blender is good, but a food processor is better. Pesto means paste. We think of pestos as spreads and sauces. Basically you can put everything in at the same time, though it's best to put your fluids in first. Run the processor on pulse. Pulse means to chop intermittently. It's a tap-tap-tap motion. Again, you need to experiment to see what textures are best for your needs. The pulse mode will give you the best results.

Roasted Pepper Pesto

2 red bell peppers
1 yellow pepper

1 Anaheim pepper

3 to 4 cloves of garlic
1 teaspoon oregano
⅓ cup basil leaves
¼ teaspoon crushed red
  peppers
1½ tablespoons virgin olive oil

1 tablespoon red wine vinegar
½ teaspoon Mrs. Dash salt
  substitute
½ teaspoon fresh cracked
  pepper

Preheat oven to 475°F. Place peppers on a baking sheet and roast for about 15 minutes, checking every few minutes. They should be blistered all over and slightly charred. Place peppers in a covered container for a few minutes and remove skins, stems and seeds. Place in a food processor with remaining ingredients and chop on pulse mode until thoroughly blended. This should take only a few pulse actions. Taste and adjust salt and pepper as needed.

Roasted Tomato Pesto

This is a unique recipe. It solves the problem of an on-hand base for pasta, dip for crudités, or spread for bread or crackers. It also works well as another layer of flavor for baked dishes such as casseroles or loaf-style dishes.

*2 pounds fresh, ripe organic
  tomatoes
2 cups fresh basil
2 tablespoons dry oregano
½ cup pine nuts
1 cup sun-dried tomatoes
6 cloves garlic
1 cup Parmesan cheese*

*⅓ cup virgin olive oil
1 teaspoon salt
1 teaspoon black pepper
4 dashes hot sauce
4 dashes Worcestershire sauce
1 tablespoon brown sugar*

Preheat oven to 425°F. Cut tomatoes in half and toss in large bowl with 1 cup basil leaves, 1 tablespoon oregano and ½ cup pine nuts. Spread one layer in a roasting pan and place in oven for about 30 minutes.

Check about every 15 minutes. Continue cooking until the skins of the tomatoes become dark red to brown. Place the mixture in a food processor and add remaining ingredients. Set processor on pulse. Pulse until the mix resembles the texture of salsa or relish.

Avocado Salsa

1 ripe avocado
1 clove garlic, minced
2 fresh tomatoes, chopped
3 green onions, sliced
¼ teaspoon cumin

1 dash toasted sesame oil
¼ cup chopped cilantro
1 dash hot sauce
Mrs. Dash salt substitute and
   pepper to taste

Peel and chop avocado. Mash in a large bowl. Stir in remaining ingredients.

I Can't Believe It's Not Egg Salad

1 package tofu, crumbled
2 tablespoons olive oil
1 teaspoon turmeric
1 tablespoon mustard
2 teaspoons fresh dill

2 ribs celery, finely chopped
2 cloves garlic, minced
2 dashes Worcestershire sauce
1 dash hot sauce

Drain tofu in a strainer. Mix with remaining ingredients. Chill for 30 minutes for best results, though it can be served immediately if need be. For something different, try adding a teaspoon or two of curry and ¼ cup chopped cilantro.

Variation: Dip for Raw or Cooked Veggies

Make the above recipe. Put salad in a food processor and chop on pulse mode a few seconds until smooth.

Chocolate Phosphate

3 tablespoons carob syrup   *8 ounces of cold seltzer*

Put syrup in a glass. Pour in liquid, stirring as you pour. Serve immediately. For a smoother texture, add in ¼ cup of Rice Dream or soy milk.

Babies and Toddlers

There is a mystical world that children allude to when it comes to their appetites. Our personal observations have led us to believe that kiddies like simply flavored foods with smooth textures. If they come upon something they like to eat, they like to have it over and over until they are saturated, and then they want to move on to something else. Because of this, our advice is to introduce the foods you think are healthful for your child on a mono-basis. This means that if a child likes cheese, don't make a cheesy casserole with lots of ingredients. Try a simple cheese quesadilla. If you want your child to eat fruit, make a smoothie. For the baby set, use your food processor to puree steamed veggies and keep it limited to one or two ingredients. Children develop their palates over time.

Please keep in mind that children also mimic their peers; in early life, this means you, the parent. If you don't eat peas, don't be surprised if your kids don't eat peas. Children are very aware and will tailor their likes and dislikes to what they observe their parents doing. In fact, children can even join in the fun of preparing foods. You're never too young to start cooking Slim & Fit, starting from scratch, or should we say by growing your own.

Growing Sprouts

Growing sprouts can be child's play, as easy as brushing their teeth twice a day. Growing sprouts is a simple process. It requires a quart-size transparent container, a strainer device, water and a little light. The timeframe is usually two to four days, depending on what type of sprouts you are growing. Generally seeds and beans that are sold for sprouting have directions on the package. The basic steps are as follows: Place one to two tablespoons of seeds or beans in the container. Cover with water and place in a cool, dark place overnight. Drain water in the morning. Add fresh water and strain again, leaving only a slight residue of moisture on the bottom. Cover the container with a piece of screen secured with a large rubber band. Place the container in a bright spot out of direct sunlight. Rinse the sprouts twice a day. Your spouts will change daily. If you started with seeds, they are mature when the first signs of leafing appears. If you started with beans, they are mature when the white root is about ¼-inch long. Again, follow the package instructions if provided.

Sprouts, by the way, are not only extremely high in nutrients; they are an excellent source of protein.

You can actually buy ready-made sprouting jars and packages of sprouting seeds in most health-food stores. Like all other nonperishable food products without preservatives, chemicals and salt, you can also purchase these things through our Slim & Fit Success Shop by calling 800-510-7973.

Sparkle's Sprout Salad

½ cup alfalfa sprouts
½ cup bean sprouts
½ cup sunflower sprouts
½ cup soy sprouts
½ cup lentil sprouts
¼ cup chopped parsley
¼ cup onion sprouts

¼ teaspoon minced garlic
¼ cup adzuki sprouts
¼ cup garbanzo bean sprouts
½ cup shredded brussels
   sprouts
½ cup soy nuts

Dressing:

⅓ cup olive oil
1 tablespoon rice vinegar
Dash of toasted sesame oil

Bit of honey
Pepper of your choice
Dash of low-salt tamari sauce

Place all ingredients in a large bowl. Pour dressing over all and toss lightly. You are done! You can also substitute your favorite dressing for the recipe given here, but, please, no hydrogenated oils or preservatives.

Miss Sparkle Britely
©1999 Christina Tsitrian

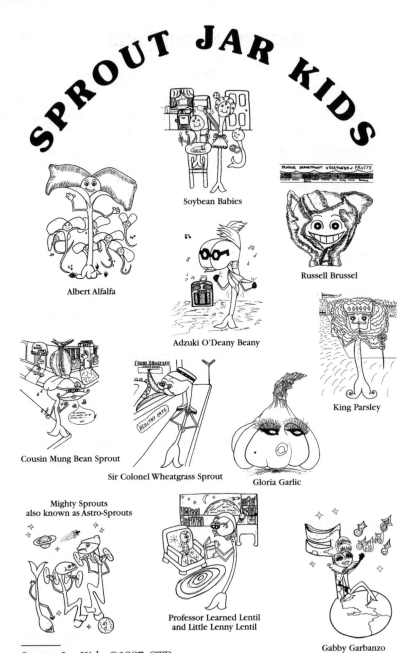

SPROUT JAR KIDS

Soybean Babies

Albert Alfalfa

Russell Brussel

Adzuki O'Deany Beany

King Parsley

Cousin Mung Bean Sprout

Sir Colonel Wheatgrass Sprout

Gloria Garlic

Mighty Sprouts
also known as Astro-Sprouts

Professor Learned Lentil
and Little Lenny Lentil

Gabby Garbanzo

Sprout Jar Kids ©1987 CTB
Created by Christina Tsitrian

SECTION II

Thinking Slim & Fit

Twelve

Boosting Your Child's Self-Esteem

Thanks to *The Beverly Hills Diet* and the incredible response it generated in the media, with celebrities and the hordes of would-be skinnies desperate to find a permanent solution to being fat, over the last twenty years my name has became a household word. Not only did the book top the *New York Times* Bestseller list and sell over one million copies, but it also propelled me into an instant celebrity with more than eight hundred radio and television shows to my credit.

What nobody knows is how much it took to compensate for the low self-esteem I'd suffered throughout my life as a result of being fat. All those old scars from all the old public humiliations associated with being a fat kid, an overweight teen and a half-fat adult held me back from being truly self-confident.

Even though I was helping clients transform themselves physically into equally gorgeous skinnies, I noticed they, too, still had trouble changing the way they perceived themselves. They, too, suffered from all the same hang-ups that being fat in a thin world had imposed.

Although I had developed a series of ploys and games designed to heighten my sense of self and create a more positive self-image, they were pretty haphazard. I made them up as I went along to "fit" occasions as they arose. When I saw how well they worked for me, I began focusing on specific problems and began creating a series of structured exercises to help my clients—as well as myself—develop a new mind-set to go along with our new bodies. What I noticed was that the clients who really made these exercises a part of their lives were infinitely more successful at maintaining their weight loss and dramatically transforming the way they felt about themselves and how they interacted with the world than those who didn't. I loved the effect these exercises had on everyone who tried them, and on myself as well, so I included them in my first book, and then improved them for *The New Beverly Hills Diet* and *The Little Skinny Companion.*

By the time *The Beverly Hills Diet* hit the bookstores and it was lights, camera and action, I felt almost as good as I looked. Almost as skinny, gorgeous and glamorous as the image I projected to the public. Of course, I was still and continue to be "a work in progress" from a psychological point of view, but I was enormously proud of all the insecurities I'd taught myself to overcome. It's interesting that even while working on this book, I've uncovered a lot of the reasons for what I consider the negative aspects of my personality that are a direct reflection of my fat childhood and the painful memories that have been buried all these years. Fortunately, now I have the tools to effectively change and eradicate their debilitating effects.

In writing this book with Dr. John, we realized that the same principles applied to kids. It isn't enough to help them achieve the bodies they've always dreamed about. Unless they feel equally confident about an inner transformation, all you've accomplished is giving a fat kid a thin body. The following nonphysical exercises are designed to help kids create an entirely new image from the inside out! There's more to eating than meets the mouth!

I'm Proud, You're Proud

More mothers of young children work outside the home than in any other period of history. This means parents are busier than ever at home, catching up with household duties, dealing with work-related chores, squeezing in time to supervise kids' homework, catch their Little League and soccer games, conferences with teachers at Back to School Night, etc. More parents are more exhausted than any other time in history. In the rush to get things done, it's easy to take for granted the little things kids achieve during the day that contribute to their positive self-image. "I'm Proud . . . You're Proud" is designed to give parents and kids a chance to acknowledge those little triumphs that might otherwise go overlooked.

For this exercise and all the others, you'll need a small notebook with dividers. The goal for each of you is to write one or two sentences each night before bed describing something the child has done that merits praise. For example, your child would write "I'm proud of me because . . ." and you would write "I'm proud of you because . . ." After each of you has finished writing, share it out loud, each reading what you have written.

These do not have to be "big" things, in fact, the smaller and more insignificant, the better. For instance, commend your child for brushing her teeth without being told. When developing a positive sense of self, little things mean a lot—especially when you start putting them all together. Encourage your child to read through the notebook on a regular basis to reaffirm how terrific he or she is.

First Thing . . . Last Thing . . . (You're the Greatest!)

In the rush to get ready for work and school, it's often hard to find time to set a positive tone for the day. This exercise is designed to do just that in a subtle, no-big-deal kind of way. However you awaken your children in the morning, whether you nudge them, nuzzle them or blow in their ear, at some point, discreetly whisper these words in their ear, "You're the greatest!" Be sure you give them the same message, the same way, when you tuck them in at night . . . even if they were naughty during the day.

You're Special Because . . .

One of the hardest things for children and adults to learn is how to accept a compliment. For children who are having a hard time at school and at home because they're overweight, seeing something positive about themselves can seem even harder. But children who get positive feedback about themselves are less likely to discount their value and less likely to turn to food for gratification.

This exercise is designed to take the focus off what a child is eating (or not eating) and put it where it belongs— on his or her uniqueness as a person. During private time, share with your child some things you find really special about him or her. Simply say, "I think you're special because . . . (you fill in the blank)." Write it in the notebook in the section reserved for that purpose. Then ask your child to pick something special about you and write it in the notebook as well.

Once the two of you have done this together, introduce this exercise to the rest of the family. Encourage your child to repeat the process with brothers, sisters, extended family and even friends: to simply go up to them and say, "I think you are really special because . . ." and then to ask them, "Now tell me something special you like about me." It might be a little difficult for your child at first, but it gets easier and easier each time he or she does it. In fact, it even becomes an enchanting game often initiated by children on their own, without their parents' prodding. Well, who doesn't like to hear good things about themselves? The role of the person being complimented is to listen, accept the positive feedback and simply say, "Thank you" and nothing else. Just accept the compliment, period; something that's not easy to do . . . or learn.

Affirmations

How many times have you heard your child make negative comments about himself or herself? "Oh, I'm so stupid. I should have gotten a better mark on that test!" or "I'm so fat and clumsy, no wonder nobody picked me for his volleyball team!" Listening to children disparage themselves can be almost as heartbreaking as hearing them report the vicious jibes other children have made about their weight.

The goal of using affirmations and their purpose is to replace this self-critical inner dialog with words saturated with sincerity, conviction and faith, so that they become highly explosive verbal atom bombs that will shatter negative thoughts and infuse a child with the pride, the power and the will to change.

The trick to affirmations is not only in the words but also in the way they are said. First, here are two affirmations to teach your child. Following is how to say them.

I'm A-Okay

"I'm perfect and getting better!" (This means you're fine as you are, but you can still strive to improve!) Your child should say this sentence each night before bedtime.

Awake and Ready

"Today I'm going to do my best, and my best today is going to be better than my best was yesterday!" Your child should say this upon arising or before leaving for school each morning.

Each of these affirmations should be said seven times. Teach your children to say their affirmations in the following way:

1. Say it very loudly the first time.
2. Less loudly the second.
3. In a normal tone of voice the third time.
4. In a soft voice the fourth time.
5. Whisper the words the fifth time.
6. Say the words to yourself the sixth and seventh times.

For Children Thirteen and Older (to Read Themselves)

In an "Affirmations" section of your notebook, make a list of the negative things you say to yourself about yourself each day. Record all the times you said, "What a jerk I am" or "How could I be so stupid." Then set aside a special time each day to reexamine them. Choose one of these negatives and turn it into a positive. For example, instead of saying, "I'm fat!" say, "I'm thin!" Instead of saying, "I'm stupid!" say, "I'm smart!" Instead of "I'm a dork!" say "I'm cool!"

Follow the guidelines on how to say affirmations, but instead of only repeating the affirmation silently two times, say each daily affirmation to yourself silently twenty times! *The power of affirmations is in the repetition.*

Then, get up and do something positive about it! Take a specific action! Make a plan to turn those fantasies into reality!

If you'd like to know more about how and why affirmations work, I would suggest the book *Scientific Healing Affirmations* by Paramahansa Yogananda, available at bookstores or by calling 323-225-2471.

Ten-Minute Mentoring

Mike Powell, who broke the world broad-jump record at the 1991 World Championships, tells this story about the way in which he developed his interest—and his ability—in jumping.

"When I was growing up, we had a long hallway that ran from one end of the house to the other. At the end was the dining room, then the living room. When I came home from school, I'd practice jumping by running through the hall, jumping across the dining room and trying to land at a red leather chair in the living room. Then I began to notice something unusual. Once I reached the chair and achieved that goal, it seemed that the chair had somehow moved farther away, so that I had to keep trying harder and harder to jump longer and longer. Years later, I discovered this was my Mother's way of encouraging me to become better and better at what I loved—broad jumping. She never yelled at me about the noise I was making. All she said about it was, 'That's great, Mike! *You can do it!*'"

Bottom line—if Mike Powell's mother had dismissed his interest in jumping and told him to go out and play, he probably would never have become one of the world's greatest broad jumpers.

In fact, when Powell was making the jump that earned

him the world record, the last thing he remembers seeing was an image of that red leather chair.

Of course you can't predict just what world records in athletics, art, literature, music, medicine, science, politics or business your own children might one day break. But you can listen, look and learn about your child's interests. If he seems fascinated by playing with melted candle wax and manipulating it into shapes, encourage his budding interest in sculpture by giving him clay to work. Talk to your young-ster. See what intrigues her; ask her what she dreams of doing and take your cue from that. Hold the image of Mike Powell's mother in your mind, and use it as an inspiration to mentor your own child.

The goal of this exercise is to discover and affirm your child's short-term goals. Whether she's in elementary or high school, ask her to describe something she'd love to do or see happen in herself. Whatever she says, even if it sur-prises you and especially if it seems totally farfetched, respond with "You can do it!"

You can do it. Trust me. There are no more powerful and empowering words in the English language, especially when you're giving your child permission to pursue a dream.

Another book by Paramahansa Yogananda that I highly recommend both you and your child—of any age—read is *Two Frogs in Trouble.* If it's not available at your bookstore, you can order it by phone from the headquarters of the organization he founded, Self-Realization Fellowship, at (323) 225-2471.

Look, See, Touch, Feel

We all do it, and we've all seen our children, spouses, friends and colleagues do it. It's called body language, and it refers to how the body builds armor to protect it under stress. It's the instinctive physical response—a tightening in the shoulder, a kink in the neck—what the body does when it tries to hold in feelings of anger, frustration, sadness and even joy and laughter. It's how little *eaters* react when someone reprimands them or says, "Don't eat that! Only slim people can eat hot fudge sundaes! Don't wear that! It makes you look fat!" Or when they react in a way that perhaps others deem inappropriate for an occasion—laughing at something no one else is laughing at, for instance. "Eaters," particularly, have a real investment in holding on to feelings because it's too painful or confusing to feel them. That's one of the reasons why we eat. I call it the mind-body split. Our hearts, not our heads, register feelings, and for the most part we just unconsciously choose not to feel them. No wonder some people slouch; others hold their neck at a slightly odd angle, while others seem to have a shoulder that looks like it has a chip on it.

The goal of Look, See, Touch, Feel is to help break down this body armor so that children feel more positive about themselves.

Whenever you talk to your child, watch how she holds herself, and how she responds physically to some of the things that are being said. Does she hunch her shoulders when she's reprimanded? Does he clench his fist when he talks about being left out of games at recess? Before the conversation ends and without making any verbal comment, in a casual kind of way simply touch your child on the spot where he or she seems to be building this structural armor. In doing this, you'll be replacing those feelings of negativity with tenderness, support and love. Over time, those hurtful feelings will start to release, and you'll begin to notice that the way your child carries himself or herself looks less tense, defiant and unhappy, and much more confident.

Trigger-Point Massage

But why not nip it in the bud before the armoring builds up? Once you've mastered the concepts behind Look, See, Touch, Feel, it's easy to move on to trigger-point massage, something I discovered almost by accident at the Pacific Athletic Club where I work out. I'd begun to notice the look of radiant well-being on the faces of clients working with personal trainer Michael Szymanski. As I was to learn firsthand (pardon the pun), their response didn't stem from the super bodies he helped them build but rather from the unique trigger-point massage à la Szymanski that he delivered between sets. Michael has prepared an easy-to-follow chart which outlines his description of his technique so you can apply his methods right at home to help your child make the connection between mind and body, to feel his or her feelings, and begin to feel sensational!

The Nurturing of Children with Touch
by Michael Szymanski

Michael Szymanski *teaches yoga and personal training at the Pacific Athletic Club in Pacific Palisades, California. He holds an advanced certification from the National Academy of Sports Medicine. He has been teaching in California and in Hawaii for the last ten years. His tech-niques are limited to only those that work.*

Michael Szymanski

For a long time now, Western medicine has assumed that newborn infants are incapable of sensing very much pain because of an underdeveloped nervous system.

There's another older school of thought, presented in book form by French obstetrician Frederick Leboyer in his book *Birth Without Violence*, which maintains that the pain and suffering which prevents us from realizing enlightenment begins with the trauma of the birth experience. This pain and suffering is literally embodied from the day we are born, creating deep-seated feelings of anxiety and abandonment and constantly affecting us every day, every hour with every breath we take.

For ten years now, I have been working with people's bodies. I have worked primarily as a personal trainer and yoga teacher, getting them into shape and adding my expertise as a massage therapist to help them heal old injuries.

I've yet to meet a client in whom I cannot identify the underlying muscular holding pattern caused by a painful birth experience and other early childhood traumas ranging from circumcision, being denied the breast in favor of bottle feeding to loud noises such as the word *No!* In some cases, as the pattern begins to loosen, the client can actually recall the particular event from early childhood.

Recently, Western science has identified a mass of gray matter located in the front portion of the brain called the amygdala. This part of the brain plays an important role in arousal, even when we are infants. Science now thinks that this is how we learn to avoid pain and dangerous situations. Even with a primitive nervous system, these often violent memories are held for decades deep in the subconscious mind.

Pediatricians are beginning to notice that muscle tension in newborns is a good indicator of how cranky a child will be. So anything to relieve bodily muscle tension is helpful.

Massage is a great way to reassure and nurture. Even unskilled hands can find tight and tender areas. A gentle back or foot rub always feels relaxing. If you are a novice, don't worry, much of the learning comes by doing and constantly gathering feedback from facial expressions and muscle tension.

To the touch, infants and young children are generally more sensitive than adults.

The tighter the muscle, the gentler the touch must be.

Trigger-point therapy is the most effective way I have found to release muscles one by one.

The first step is to locate the trigger point, which exits a band or spot of tight fibers in the muscle. The body is wrapped in up to three layers of muscle, so they can be at depth. Thumb pressure is applied to the trigger until it releases. First press lightly, then gradually increase the pressure until the trigger point melts away.

Pressing too hard too soon will only cause the trigger to tighten more. So go slow and look for feedback (face and body tension).

Consult the chart for locations of common trigger-point locations. They do vary from person to person.

Trigger-Point Location Chart

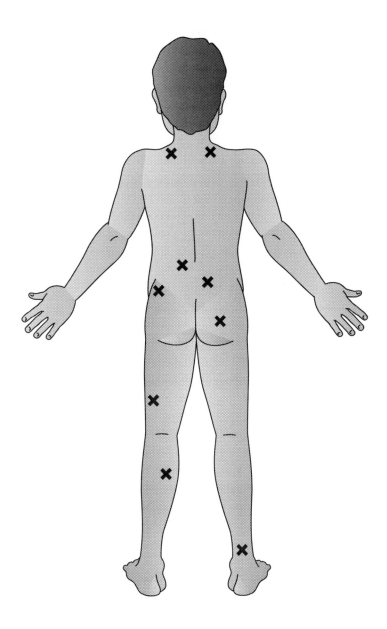

SECTION III

Moving
Slim & Fit

Thirteen

Work It Out with Thea!

The local newspaper published for my small community of Pacific Palisades runs a full page of ads for kids' exercise programs. There's Child's World, Kids' Universe and Kids' Club, all offering afterschool physical activities for kids. Then there's tennis camp, baseball camp and the UCLA Bruin summer camp that combines it all—baseball, basketball, football, golf, gymnastics, soccer, swimming, tennis, throwing, softball, volleyball and water polo! And if that's not enough, parents can hire a personal trainer for their kids!

And the media says kids today are overweight because they don't get enough exercise! Something is definitely wrong with this picture!

When I was growing up, if you wanted to participate in an organized afterschool activity you had two choices—the playground or the bowling alley. To get there, however, I walked or rode my bike. Yes, kids today are getting infinitely more exercise. What they're not getting is activity—

they don't walk to the corner store for Mom; they don't ride their bikes to the library; they don't get to pick up a softball game in the empty lot.

Kids don't want to exercise. They want to have fun. Exercise today has become something that people do with a sharply focused intention. For adults, the goal is burning fat by getting the heart rate up so they can lose weight. For kids, exercise has become another highly structured activity that's often an extension of the school day. They go home from class to play soccer, T-ball or gymnastics.

How do they get from school to these mini-Olympics? Do they ride their bikes, skateboards, run? Of course not. They're driven in Mom's SUV!

Whatever happened to the days that families played together—dancing crazily around the living room for the sheer joy of being alive? Shooting hoops outside with the whole family? Riding bikes on a Sunday afternoon down to the park? In this craze to exercise, we've somehow left out two essentials: fun and family!

Welcome to Work It Out with Thea! It's a program that works out all the major muscle groups, pumps up the cardio-vascular system, teaches coordination, conditioning and endurance while sharpening the mind's ability to stay focused. It's fun, fabulous and fantastic not only for your child, but for the entire family to do together! The days are structured to vary in length to keep your eager little "eater" hungering not for more food but for more of a chance to work it out!

When you begin Thea's program, aim to just have fun. Just do what you both can do; don't try to be perfect; laugh and experiment with how your bodies perform, and, of course, encourage your child to do the same. What we don't want is for kids to grow frustrated with what they can't do. That will only make them hungry. So relax and watch how your relationship with your children and their relationship to you and also to their own body will blossom as you get slim and fit together while you Work It Out with Thea!

Thea recommends her program for children between the ages of six and twelve. For toddlers two to four, she has developed carefully thought-out, though seemingly unstructured, song and dance theme classes that really keep the kids moving and having fun for thirty minutes while developing association skills. Using popular music that the kids know and can relate to, Thea becomes the Pied Piper. She creates games to play that are accompanied by specific songs. The children play common kid games like hide and seek or musical chairs, for instance, and always to the same song. They may use props, like balls to play catch, bounce on their feet or jump over, or exercise mats to "swim" on or "jump into the water from." By always using the same song for the same activity, children know when they hear it what they are going to do and what is expected of them.

Gymboree Play Programs (800-520-PLAY) has over four hundred centers around the world. They offer a full range of developmentally appropriate classes with the emphasis on developing more skills, concentration, rhythm and eye-hand coordination for children as young as six months old and as old as age three. It's a great afternoon outing!

What about your five- and six-year-olds? Introduce them to the Fun Fitness Routine, but go very slowly and *laugh a lot* at what you and your child can't do yet. They are still a little young to have the concentration and coordination skills required for some of the routines, but with patience and a sense of humor, they will work up to them. What a sense of pride and accomplishment their achievements will engender. This is also just the perfect age to introduce them to Dance Alive! (chapter 14) to begin moving and understanding their body and their connection to it.

A Word from Thea

Thea White Riches

It took a visit to my daughter's elementary school watching the P.E. coach execute the same exercises time after time to realize how behind we are in motivating kids in physical fitness.

How many jumping jacks, trips around the track, or touching the toes up and down to realize—this is boring! Didn't we do that as youngsters? Should we maybe alter or supplement this strategic approach with a more motivational approach? Reading articles claiming obesity in children is getting worse not better, and seeing the rise of children's computer time not only in the home but at school draws me to the conclusion our children's nutrition and fitness well-being is not being met. There are sport-related activities for children who are genetically sporty or even active, but there are many average children whose genetic make-up comes from parents who are struggling with the same issues they are.

Living my life in a dance and exercise world, I have seen efforts in enlightening the adult on the latest breakthroughs of exercise in health clubs and gyms around the world. I've always wondered why this information was not brought to children through physical education programs at school.

For children, nutritional education only came through the trials and errors of the adults. In fitness how can we expect children to be motivated through the same proxy? Preschoolers have a chance with song and stories through animated characters or bigger-than-life prehistoric creatures. What happens after six into puberty?

Spending a lot of time educating myself in workshops, seminars and becoming an accredited fitness instructor along with all the top-of-the-line instructors in the world, I've come to know the success of accomplishing a change for our children's fitness regime. It's the creativity, the motivation and the passion of an instructor, especially a motivational instructor who knows how to conduct a class for the appropriate age group and who can motivate that group to want to do it again and again! Sometimes the answer is not only the number of letters you have after your name, or the latest piece of equipment, or the latest new fad on the market. The answer is the appointed few, who step forward, who have been called to *deliver* the goods, because it's what they were designed to do.

When designing my kids' club program at the Pacific Athletic Club, I had the program already visualized in my head. I saw a full spectrum of the broadest scope in fitness today, utilizing what is proven to be beneficial in the way of improving flexibility, stamina, cardiovascular endurance, muscle strength, muscle tone, focus, mental alertness and just plain fun. I've incorporated yoga, kickboxing, treadmill step, and hip-hop into a comprehensive structure.

I saw the children waiting to be stimulated with every piece of equipment in the gym. Their eyes widened when I took out the boxing gloves and shields to kickbox. When warming them up I used choreographed movement, which they had to learn first and then attempt to music. They (especially the boys) were emancipated. Completing a goal of forty-five minutes with them changing from one element to the next, they had no idea they were working out. They did not want to stop and voiced, "When are we going to do this again, Ms. Thea?"

The only true test of success in a fitness program is the test of time. It's been a daily ritual working two schools in the Pacific Palisades and PAC's Kids' Club. I know I have something that works and is here to stay. Having children look forward to P.E. at school or attending a Kids' Club program is all worth the time and energy I've invested in designing something fun and motivating. I just thank the heavenly Father above for all of his gifts that he bestowed on us and for allowing me to acknowledge what he has given me. God bless the children and may he let them move more freely.

When Judy Mazel came to me and asked would I contribute information on a children's fitness program for a book she was involved with, little did she know what chest of treasures was about to open. I have longed to deliver the vast ideas and knowledge to the public in regards to children and fitness. How was I going to integrate experience and choreography in a text? Well, to start, we both agreed motivation was a key factor in keeping a child's attention and interest so we adopted the partner system. Not only will the child benefit from this workout, but now a friend or parent will, too! Now that we have a fun set-up, I thought of how the warm-up should be a fun routine to learn while preparing the major muscle groups for exercise. Rhythmic reaches and stretches for the upper body incorporated with forward flexion and squats for the lower body would increase the blood flow for the muscles involved and prepare the heart for cardiovascular conditioning. Then formulating movements with simple side steps with turns continues the fitness process toward an aerobic workout. In maintaining the aerobic conditioning, I choreographed simple and fun across-the-floor moves that children love to do. While enjoying these nonstop drills, the children also learn coordination and syncopated movement. Next, I wanted to incorporate strength moves for muscle conditioning and endurance. Kickboxing is so popular and caters to muscle conditioning in the upper and lower body. I developed a series of combinations derived from cardio-kickboxing classes, which worked the best.

Rounding the program to increase flexibility, heighten mental focus, and calm this now very motivated and excited child, yoga asanas seemed to be the most beneficial. Now I was ready to take this new program to the public schools in my community and test the results. Well, the results are in, and the tests were positive. Now, here it is for you and your child. I look forward to hearing about your success.

Fun Fitness in 28 Days

	Day 1	Day 2	Day 3	Day 4	Day 5	Day 6	Day 7
WEEK I Warm-Up Hip-Hop	1. Arm stretch; side stretch; around the world; chest back stretch; shoulder rotation	2. Reach for stars; side-tap march; march side-to-side	3. Combine days 1 and 2.	4. Slides; slides with power; out jump in; grapevine; runaways	5. Repeat day 1, plus long leg kicks; one knee jumps; bunny sequence.	6. Combine days 4 and 5.	7. Combine days 1, 2, 4, 5.
	Day 8	**Day 9**	**Day 10**	**Day 11**	**Day 12**	**Day 13**	**Day 14**
WEEK II Kickboxing	8. Punches 1-2; punches in sync, punch squat drop; punches 1, 2, 3, 4 with 2 squat drops.	9. Punch 1, 2 with knee; punch sync with knee; punches 1, 2, 3, 4.	10. Combine days 8 and 9.	11. Repeat day 8; add punch, kick, squat.	12. Repeat day 9; add punch, punch, kick, squat.	13. Repeat day 12; add punch, punch, kick, squat, kick.	14. Combine days 11 and 12; add punch, punch, kick, squat, kick, punch, punch.
	Day 15	**Day 16**	**Day 17**	**Day 18**	**Day 19**	**Day 20**	**Day 21**
WEEK III Yoga	15. Sun salutation.	16. Half-moon.	17. Combine days 15 and 16.	18. Forward bending.	19. Repeat day 18 twice; tree.	20. Sitting side stretch.	21. Combine days 15, 16, 17, 18, 19 and 20.
	Day 22	**Day 23**	**Day 24**	**Day 25**	**Day 26**	**Day 27**	**Day 28**
WEEK IV Putting It All Together	22. Combine days 1, 2, 4 and 5.	23. Combine days 11, 12 and 13.	24. Combine days 15, 16, 18, 19, 20.	25. Combine days 22 and 23.	26. Combine days 22 and 24.	27. Combines days 23 and 24.	28. Combine days 22, 23 and 24.

Fun Fitness Routine

Week I: Aerobics and Hip-Hop

DAY 1

Arm Stretch

Stretch your right arm up, then down. Stretch your left arm up, then down. Stretch both arms up, then down. Arms at side, tuck head and roll body down from waist, touch floor. Roll straight up from waist—arms out to the side. Shift rib cage left-right, left-right. Repeat from beginning four times.

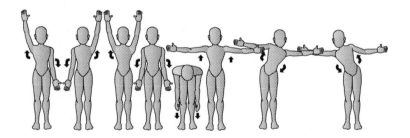

Side Stretch

With left hand on hip, stretch your right arm up over your head. Stretch to the left pulsing four times: 1 and 2 and 3 and 4. Stand straight. With right hand on hip, lift your arm up over head. Stretch to the right pulsing four times: 1 and 2 and 3 and 4. Repeat four times.

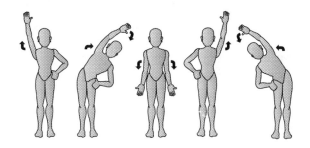

Around the World

With left hand on hip, stretch your right arm up over head. Stretch to the left, drop your head, slightly bend knees and roll down, making a semi-circle with the upper body. Place hands on knees. Stand straight up. Return your arm to your side. Raise arms out. Repeat four times. Change arms: right hand on hip stretching to the left. Repeat four times.

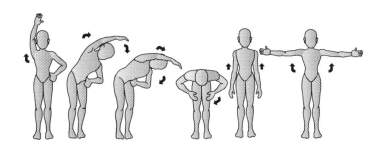

Chest Back Stretch

Stand with your arms straight out to side. Rapidly scissor arms right over left, left over right, alternating sixteen times. Place arms to side. Repeat four times.

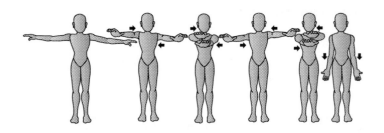

Shoulder Rotation

Extend your arms out. Clasp fingers. Drop head down to knees, keeping hands clasped and reaching for the floor. Come up to standing with arms clasped overhead. Unclasp hands and stretch your arms straight out to side.

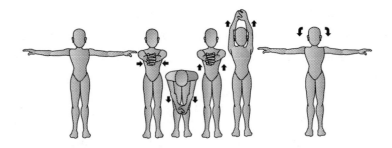

DAY 2

Reach for the Stars

Start with arms at side, feet shoulder-width apart. Reach right arm across your body and up to the sky, shifting weight to the left, then repeat in other direction. Repeat sixteen times.

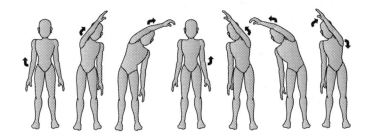

Step-Tap

Drop your arms down to side. Step to side with right leg. Bring left foot (leg) to meet it. Step back to left side. Bring right foot to meet left. Repeat sixteen times side to side.

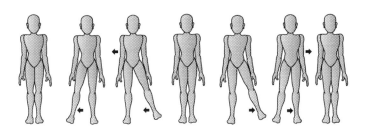

March

March in place forty beats, arms swinging at sides. Keep marching and bring arms up over head, then out to side (shoulder level), down to side, then hands on hips. Repeat marching hands up, out, down on hip forty times.

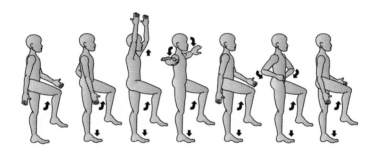

Side to Side

Start with your arms straight out at your side. Step out to your side with left leg, while lifting arms straight out at your side. Cross your right leg over your left leg, while rounding your arms in front of your chest, placing your hands together in fist. Unwind your body by spinning to the left. Jump up and face front.

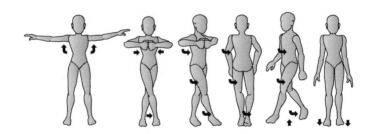

DAY 3

Combine days 1 and 2, but cut the repetitions in half.

DAY 4

Hip-Hop—Fancy Footwork

Slides

Stand with your arms straight out to the side. Slide sideways in one direction, four slides, and slide back, four slides to starting point. Repeat four times.

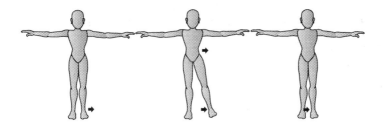

Slides with Power

Start with arms straight out to side. Slide two times to the right. Cross arms over chest. Jump in the air and spin in a circle, land facing forward with arms stretched out to side. Do two more times in the same direction. Stop and slide back four slides to starting point.

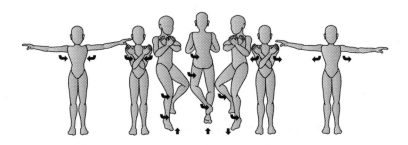

Out Jump In

Start with arms at side. Step your right foot out to side while raising your arms straight out to sides. Jump up with left foot, then right. Repeat four times. Change directions and legs, and repeat four times.

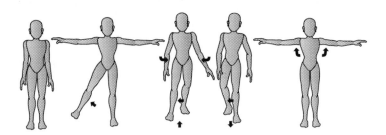

Grapevine

Keep your arms straight down to the sides. Cross right leg in front of left. Left leg steps out to the side. Right leg crosses behind left leg. Left leg steps out to the side. Repeat eight times and change legs.

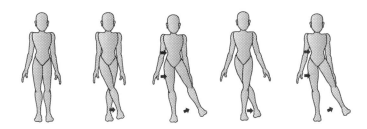

Runaways

Run forward four steps. Stop with both feet together. Bend knees. Reach up and jump up. Upon landing, run four more paces. Repeat jump up, turn and go back in other direction. Repeat four times.

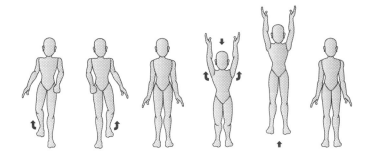

DAY 5

Repeat day 1, but cut repetitions in half. Add the following:

Long Leg Kicks

Start with arms out to sides. Walk and kick up with straight legs as high as possible, going four steps. Turn around and repeat, going back to starting point.

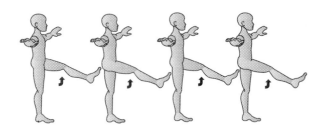

One-Knee Jumps

Step forward with your right foot. Jump up with left knee and reach overhead with right arm, pointing left arm straight out to side. Repeat with other side.

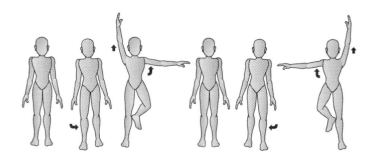

Bunny Sequence

Start with feet together. Bend knees and swing arms behind. Reach up with your arms and jump up. Come down with bent knees, torso forward and arms stretching back. Repeat four times.

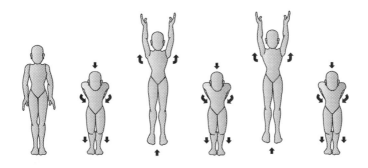

DAY 6

Repeat days 4 and 5

DAY 7

Repeat days 1, 2, 4 and 5, doing half the repetitions.

Week II: Kickboxing

DAY 8

Punch 1, 2

Stand with your legs apart, arms bent. Clench your fists under your chin as if you are going to punch someone. Extend your right arm across your chest in a punch. Bring back to center. Pause, then do same with your left arm. Repeat twenty-five times in single time counting: 1 and 2 and 1 and 2 and . . .

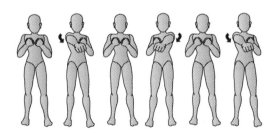

Punch in Sync

Stand in same position as Punch 1, 2, but the rhythm changes. Punch right, left, no pause in between. Pause after two punches. Repeat twenty-five times.

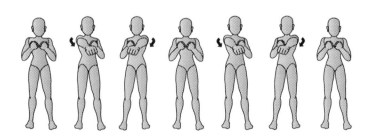

Punch and Squat Drop

Punch left arm, right arm, squat, stand up, pause. Repeat five times.

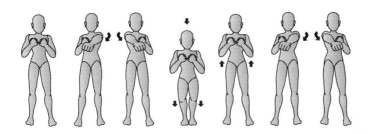

Punch 1, 2, 3, 4

Four repetitive punches: left, right, left, right. Pause. Repeat ten times and end with two four-punch squat drops.

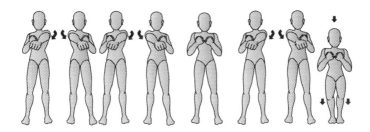

DAY 9

Punch 1, 2 with Knee

Leading with your right hand, punch, pause, punch with your left hand, pause, bring your right knee to your chest. Repeat with other side. Repeat series eight times.

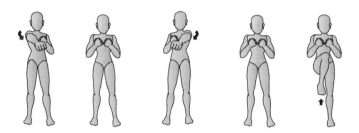

Punch Sync with Knee

Punch 1, 2, leading with right then left (no pause between punches). Then right knee up. Repeat on same side eight times, then repeat on other side eight times.

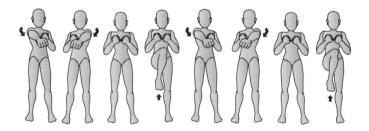

Punch Sync 1, 2, 3, 4 with Two Squat Drops

Punch right, left, right, left (no pause), then do two squat drops. Repeat eight times.

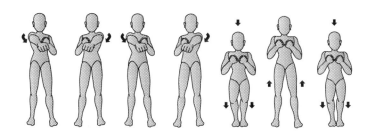

DAY 10

Repeat days 8 and 9. If necessary, cut repetitions in half.

DAY 11

Repeat day 8. Add:

Punch, Kick, Squat

Stand with your hands in fists in front of your chest. Punch out with your right hand. Bend your right knee to your chest. Extend your foot out straight. Bring leg down and return to standing squat, then immediately kick out leg as you return to standing. Repeat eight times on each leg, one leg at a time. Repeat other leg eight times.

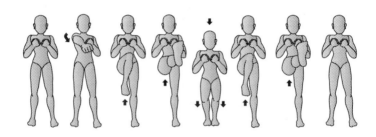

DAY 12

Repeat day 9. Add:

Punch, Punch, Kick, Squat

Punch right, punch left, kick right, squat. Repeat on same side eight times, then do eight repetitions on the left side.

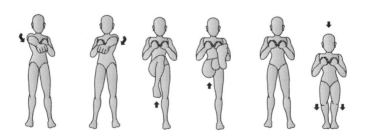

DAY 13

Repeat day 12. Add:

Punch, Punch, Kick, Squat, Kick

Punch right, punch left, kick right, squat, kick left. Repeat eight times. Do eight repetitions on the other side.

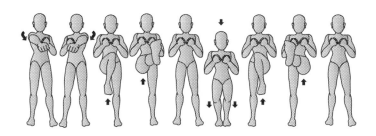

DAY 14

Repeat days 11 and 12. Add:

Punch, Punch, Kick, Squat, Kick, Punch, Punch

Punch right, punch left, kick right, squat, kick left, punch left, punch right. Repeat eight times.

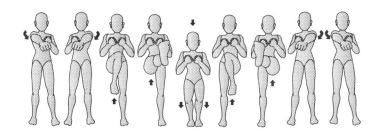

Week III: Yoga

DAY 15

Sun Salutation

Start with feet together and arms at side. Raise arms up overhead, palms forward. Lean upper body back, tilt head back. Tilt head forward, lean upper body forward, reach arms down to touch floor while tucking head. Bend to squat, hands alongside feet on floor. Reach right leg straight back. Bring hands up overhead, balance on left foot. Hands come back on the floor. Bring right leg back so right foot meets left foot in squat. Tuck head, raise hips up with head to knees. Roll up with arms moving straight in front, then overhead. Repeat, bringing left leg back. Do four repetitions on each leg.

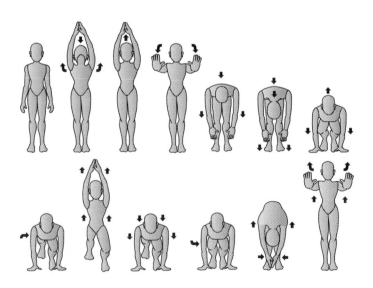

DAY 16

Half-Moon

Reach your arms over your head, clasping hands. Try to squeeze your ears with your arms. Bend sideways from the waist to the right. Hold for a four-count. Straighten with arms over head. Bend to the left for a four-count. Straighten with arms over head. Arms remaining overhead, drop your head back. Reach arms back over your head, bending your body gently back from the waist. Bring arms up and overhead, then down in front of body and try to touch the floor. Come back to standing, arms to side. Repeat four times. Hold each position for a slow count of four.

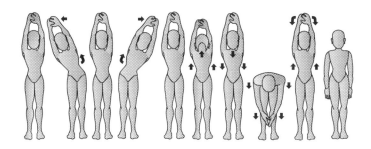

DAY 17

Repeat days 15 and 16.

DAY 18

Forward Bending

Stand with your feet shoulder-width apart, your arms at your side. Reach behind, clasping hands and opening chest. Pull arms down. Look up. Neck and head stretch back and come forward from waist as far as possible, arms coming up behind you, eyes looking straight ahead. Hold for a count of eight. Come up from waist, arms to side. Stand straight. Count to eleven and repeat six times.

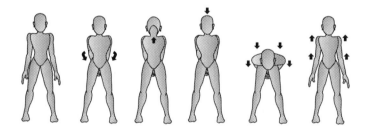

DAY 19

Do two repetitions of day 18. Add:

Tree

Stand with your arms up overhead. Clasp your hands. Balance on left leg. Slide right leg up. Rest sole of right foot at side of knee of left leg and hold for a count of four. Repeat other side. Pause and count to eleven. Repeat three times.

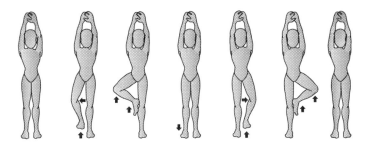

DAY 20

Sitting Side Stretch

Sit on the floor with your legs apart as far as they will go. Reach arms up over head. Clasp hands together over head. Bend from the waist to the left, trying to touch forehead to knee, and hold for a four-count. Come up to straight position. Walk hands forward flat on floor with head down as far as you can go. Hold for a four-count. Come up straight. Repeat side stretch to right, holding for a four-count. Pause in a reclining position for an eleven-count, then sit up and touch your toes. Repeat four times.

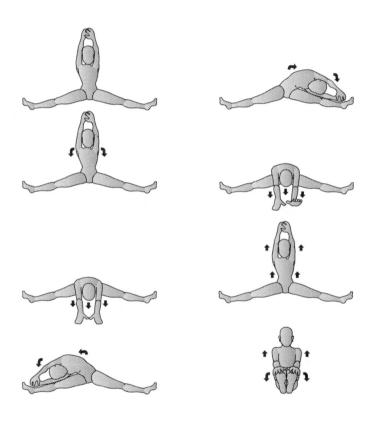

DAY 21

Repeat days 15, 16, 17, 18 and 19.

Week IV: Putting It All Together

DAY 22

Repeat days 1 to 7.

DAY 23

Repeat days 8 to 19.

DAY 24

Repeat days 15 to 21.

DAY 25

Repeat days 22 and 23.

DAY 26

Repeat days 22 and 24.

DAY 27

Repeat days 23 and 24.

DAY 28

Repeat days 22, 23 and 24.

Fourteen

Dance Alive™!

Dance Alive! came into my life when I'd thought I'd gone as far as I could in transforming the way I presented myself to the world. If I'd had any body armoring left after spending the last twenty years experiencing the plethora of body therapies available, including Reichian Therapy, Rolfing, Bioenergetics and Trigger-Point Massage, among others, the lovely, the brilliant, the creative Mariane Karou and her wonderful program completed the process. Now I not only feel my mind-body split is healed, I'm also having the time of my life! I count the moments until 9:30 A.M. Friday morning when I can get into Mariane Karou's Dance Alive! and do my thing. That's exactly what's in store for you, your child and even your entire family. It's all here in perfect, easy and fun-to-follow steps. Children of *any* age can follow it once they are walking, of course.

Like anything that dramatically challenges preconceived ideas, Dance Alive! may seem a little overwhelming. It is not as confusing as it first appears to be. In fact, it's not confusing at all. As you read through the exercises and Mariane's explanations, you'll find Dance Alive! easy, fun and compelling. Don't rush into it with unrealistic expectations. Go slowly. You don't have to do all the exercises the first time and don't expect perfection. Be willing to trust yourself to try new approaches. Make as many mistakes as you have to. You can correct them as you go. That, after all, is how we learn.

Dance Alive! is a simple, delightful way to relate to your child and for your children to begin to relate to their bodies and to other kids. Don't worry about doing the exercises exactly as they're described; you can't make a mistake. There really is no *really* right or wrong way to do them. Use them as a springboard to jump into being slim and fit. Encourage your children to trust themselves, to just let go and discover new levels of expression, and you do the same thing. So, just relax, turn on the music and have fun! Get to know your children in a new way. Even better, involve the rest of the family in this new New-Age parlor game!

Now I'll turn the floor over to Mariane.

Dance Alive™! Kids by Mariane Karou

Mariane Karou

All people have energy. While young, we develop patterns that are difficult to change as we grow older. The body is more adaptable and fluid, and the structures we create as children become imprinted in our nervous system and brain. We carry these patterns throughout our adult life. Thus, how we are trained is very important .

The Dance Alive! method trains the body, the brain and the nervous system in basic patterns that will serve children their entire lives. The Dance Alive! system is based on right and left hemisphere balance and integration. The left side of the brain (the analytical, logical, reasoning and rational center) and the right side (the intuitive, nonlinear, creative center), when working together, create a well-balanced and healthy mind and body. This system, though based in physical movement, is designed to accelerate the function of the individual as a whole. Imprinting the nervous system is invaluable, for these imprints are the basic programs on which we run our lives as adults.

Children are in great need of a way to direct their energy that allows for their creativity while at the same time develops inner discipline. They do not know what to do with the abundance of energy they have, and they need direction. Adults are often overwhelmed with their energy and do not know how to direct children's energy without damaging the children's spirits. Children need to learn how to manage and direct their energy so they can live in the world effectively. When I began training students in movement, I saw extreme personalities and behaviors. I found that movement created a balance in the students.

The shy introvert became more assertive, outgoing and gregarious. The aggressive, hyperactive child became more calm, relaxed and responsive. The irrational, hysterical child became more rational. The overly analytical child became more creative. This inspired me to continue to pursue my explorations with movement.

I continued to find that movement consistently created a centered and balanced person. I went on to develop the Dance Alive! method. This method is a comprehensive system that includes right/left brain balance and integration, balance between expression and containment, balance between spontaneity and structure, and the development of a variety of skills. Children will: learn to activate, manage and direct energy; develop strength and fluidity; increase concentration and creativity; enhance body image and self-confidence; develop teamwork skills; learn to lead—be clear, assertive, directive and focused; and learn to follow—be receptive, responsive, adaptable and flexible.

This is a fun, creative and challenging program for all

ages. Creativity is natural and something everyone is born with it. Creativity can be encouraged or suppressed. The value of encouraging creativity is that creative people have many more options and choices in life (E.g., if you have a problem and have only one way to solve it, you are very limited. If you take a creative approach, you can come up with countless ways of solving the problem.) In addition, being creative is fun and challenging and keeps us very alert. When we work creatively together, life is more enjoyable together.

Through movement, I can encourage endless creativity in the individual. The movement style we will be using to enhance creativity is fluid movement. Water can always move in any direction. As you learn to move like water, you develop the ability to be adaptable, versatile, flexible and fluid like the octopus is in the water.

A structure is a container for movement that takes place inside of it. For example, your body is a structure. All structures are made of parts that make the whole. All parts are separated by a boundary or limit. All structures have boundaries within them. Boundaries separate one area from another, one movement from the next and one person from another. Through movement, you can learn to gain ownership of boundaries and learn to respect your own and another's boundaries. You can start a movement and stop a movement. This clearly separates one movement from the next. You can focus internally on one part of the body and then on another part. You can gain control of your own body and learn to synchronize with an outer direction or rhythm. Unless you can be aware of separation, you can never experience union. All this will benefit you and, of course, your child.

The integration of structure and fluidity is vital to having a healthy relationship with yourself and with others. Structure allows for clear definition and identity. Fluidity allows for trust and union. The combination of these two styles of movement and thinking develops a self-confident individual capable of maintaining fulfilling relationships.

Throughout the exercises, I will help you define and demonstrate working within boundaries. It is through creating boundaries that we develop structure.

The Dance Alive! method also includes a mental and emotional focus. The mental focus directs the mind in a positive direction. The body is effected and responds to the thoughts you have. It allows you to notice thoughts that tear you down or build you up; thoughts that build/stimulate energy flow and strengthen you; thoughts that tear down/block energy flow and weaken you. The mental focus is designed to focus your mind prior to the exercise. While doing the exercise, put attention on the kinesthetic feeling.

The emotional focus allows you and your child to feel your feelings and include them as you focus on the movement. All feelings are felt sensations in the body. If feelings are not directed, they become repressed in the body, lodging and freezing in the musculature and cells, thus creating rigidity, excess tension and body armor. If feelings are released without management, they take over, overloading the system, thus creating overindulgence, too little tension and lack of cohesion. The physical and emotional structures are connected in the body. Allowing the feelings throughout the exercises validates them. It is not necessary to dissect, analyze or understand them. It is important simply to feel and acknowledge and not get lost in the expression of them. This keeps the mind and body balanced. Thus, it is essential to be able to feel your feelings, allow them, direct and manage them so that the physical, emotional and mental body can work as a team.

The Dance Alive! method is accompanied by different types of music. Music is a very important part of every exercise. Music has a dramatic effect on the body, inspiring the body to move; on the emotions, evoking feelings; and on the mind, stimulating the right/left hemispheres of the brain. Music can either create a very balanced effect or it can stimulate a particular area of the body/mind that you want to stimulate. Each exercise is designed to be accompanied by a specific type of music. I am suggesting different types of music, each with a specific purpose. These specific pieces of music help facilitate each exercise. In addition, I suggest specific musical artists and selections. These suggestions can be replaced with other music of the appropriate types and can be updated.

The Dance Alive! method consists of five basic type of movements.

1. Soft Liquid—fluid subtle

2. Reach Out—fluid stretching

3. Power Up—fluid isometrics

4. Gotta Move—fluid active, repetitive and random

5. Dance Alive—integration

The person directing the exercise should read the dialogue (script). Repeat it slowly and melodically, gently stretching it out and repeating it so that you are doing the exercise for about three minutes. Now that doesn't mean you have to stop at three minutes. You can and should keep doing it as long as it continues to be fun!

Soft Liquid

Soft Liquid is felt by tuning into a subtle sensation in the body and moving your awareness from one sensation to the next while moving incrementally through your body in the area where your awareness lies. It can appear as a fluid, gentle, rolling or undulating movement. It can be experienced anywhere throughout the body.

The body is made up of approximately 80 percent water. In soft liquid movement, we move through the fluid systems of the body. As water always moves around all obstacles and forms and adapts itself to whatever is in its way, such is the same as fluid movement. We can move around tension, and through tissue, muscle and bone. There is no push nor pull in this form of movement. It requires that you allow, receive, include and flow with the natural design within the organism.

Purpose: This exercise deeply relaxes the entire body through fluid movement.

Exercise 1: Soft Liquid—Individual

Mental Focus: I listen to the feelings inside my body as I move.

Suggested Music: *Shamanic Dream* by Anugama, *Songs from a Secret Garden* by Secret Garden

Position: Standing, feet flat on the floor.

Method:

1. Move your knees very softly and gently in any direction, as if they were a wave on the ocean.

2. Move your hips very softly and gently in any direction, allowing the knees to move, too.

3. Move your ribcage very softly and gently in any direction, allowing the knees and hips to move, too.

4. Move your chest and shoulders very softly and gently in any direction, allowing the knees, hips and ribcage to move, too.

5. Move your neck and head very softly and gently in any direction, allowing the knees, hips, ribcage, chest and shoulders to move, too.

6. Move your arms very softly and gently in any direction, allowing the knees, hips, ribcage, chest, shoulders, neck and head to move, too.

7. Follow the feeling inside your body as you move.

Exercise 1: Dialogue (Script to Say During the Exercise)

Stand with your feet flat on the floor, as if they were stuck there by glue. Let your eyes close and begin to listen inside your body. Notice how your breath moves in and out of your body. Notice where it moves inside your body. Does it move into your chest or belly? Just notice your breath and allow it be just as it is right now. Now, begin to let your body move very softly, very slowly. Let your body move in any way that feels good to you. Allow your body to soften and relax. Move as if you were a wave on the ocean, very soft, very slow, very gentle. Good.

Now bring your attention to your knees. Let your knees move as if they were a wave on the ocean. Softly, softly. Letting the knees move very softly. Good. Let your knees move in a way that feels really good to your knees. Good.

Now, let's bring your attention into your hips. Let your hips move very softly, slowly, very gently. Feel inside your hips. How do your hips want to move? Let your hips move in any way that feels really good to your hips. Good. Keep going. Softly, softly. Feel the hips loosening. Begin to notice how the legs and knees want to move with the hips. Allow them to move with the hips. Feel how they move together while you move softly and slowly. Good.

Now bring your attention into your ribcage. Let your ribcage move very softly, very slowly. Feeling inside your ribcage. How does your ribcage want to move? Feel your ribcage softening. Good. Keep going. Softening, very slowly. Notice how your hips, legs and knees want to move with your ribcage. Feel how they move together. Good.

Now, bring your attention up into your chest, moving very softly. Feel how your chest wants to move. Very softly, very slowly. As if you were a wave on the ocean. Good. Allow your shoulders to move with your chest. Softening, softening. Notice how your ribcage, hips, legs and knees want to move with your chest and shoulders. Feel how they move together very softly. Good. Keep going. Softening, as if you were a wave on the ocean. Now let your neck and head begin to move very softly with the chest and shoulders. Following the feeling inside the chest. Good. Feel the neck and head soften and relax. No pushing, no pulling, just softness. Good. Let your arms begin to move with your shoulders and chest. Following the chest, feeling inside your body. Notice how every part of your body is moving together. Good.

Keep moving, as if you were a wave on the ocean. Feel how your body moves from the inside. Feel how soft and liquid you are. Very good. And slowly let yourself come back to starting position. Let yourself be still and feel the sensations inside your body. Feel your breath moving through your body. Feel how soft and relaxed your body is. Good.

Exercise 2: Soft Liquid—Partner (Could be a sibling, friend, Mom or Dad. When an adult partners with a child, it is best for the adult to do it on their knees so they can be the same height.)

Mental Focus: I receive your energy. Thank you.

Suggested Music: Same as Exercise 1

Position: Facing your partner.

Method:

1. Bring your hands up to shoulder level and let your hands touch very softly.

2. Move your hands very softly and gently together like a wave.

3. Allow your arms and shoulders to move softly with your hands.

Exercise 2: Dialogue (Script)

Now, we're going to move the same way with our partner. Say hello to your partner. Good. Now, stand facing each other. Keep your feet firmly on the floor and bring your hands up to shoulder height. Let your hands touch very lightly palm to palm. Just feel your partner's hands. No pushing or pressing. Just feel their hands meeting your hands. Good. Now slowly begin to move your hands, keeping in contact with your partner's hands. Let your hands move together very softly. Good. Let your body move very softly, too. Feel how your partner's hands are moving. Feel how your hands are moving. Feel how your hands are moving together. Good. Keep going. Moving very softly, very slowly, as if you were a wave on the ocean. Good. Keep going. Softly, slowly. Feeling how your hands are moving together. Good. And, slowly let your hands come back to starting position. Just let your hands be still and feel your partner's hands touching yours. Good.

Exercise 3: Soft Liquid—Partner

Mental Focus: I receive your energy. Thank you.

Suggested Music: Same as Exercise 1

Position: Back to back with your partner.

Method:

1. Let your backs touch softly.
2. Move your backs like a wave together.
3. Do not bump against each other. Keep your backs touching softly.

Exercise 3: Dialogue (Script)

Now, turn back to back with your partner. Keeping your feet flat on the floor, let your backs touch. Make sure your backs are soft and liquid. No bumping or pushing. Just soft and liquid. Imagine you are a wave on the ocean and begin to let your backs move together very softly. Feel how your partner's back is moving. Feel how your back is moving. Feel how your backs are moving together. Good. Keep going. Moving very slowly, very softly, as if you were a wave on the ocean. Feeling how your backs are moving together softly. Good. Slowly come back to starting position and just feel your partner's back against yours. Feel your back against your partner's. Feel your backs meeting each other. Good. Thank your partner.

Note: Watch and use the movements to encourage your verbal directions to stretch the exercise to about three minutes.

Reach Out

Reach Out is felt by gently unwinding the body and reaching through the core into and through the extremities. It's a form of fluid stretching movements that expand the length and width throughout the body. The connective tissue wraps itself around the bones and muscle. Through softening and expanding the connective tissue, you unwind the tensions and create less density throughout the body. This then allows you to move into the very edges of your movement, expanding your capacity to open and lighten the body.

By working through the connective tissue, you connect the fluid system with the muscular system. This produces an organic sense of connection.

Purpose: This exercise expands the entire body through a fluid stretching routine.

Exercise 1: Reach Out—Individual

Mental Focus: I am reaching out into the world.

Suggested Music: *The Light of the Spirit* by Kitaro, *MCMXC A.D.* by Enigma

Position: Feet flat on floor, as if they were stuck to it.

Method:

1. Move body slowly and softly in any direction.

2. Reach out in the direction your body is going until you feel like you can't go any farther.

3. Let your body curve and move, reaching out in a new direction. Continue moving and reaching for a few more minutes.

4. Remember to keep your feet flat on the floor.

Exercise 1: Dialogue (Script)

Stand with your feet flat on the floor, as if they were stuck there by glue. Let your eyes close and begin to move your body very softly as if it were a wave on the ocean. Good.

Now begin to reach out in any direction. Allow your body to stretch in that direction. Feel your body stretching and lengthening. Keep going, keep reaching in that direction until you feel like you can't go any farther. Then, let your body curve and reach out in a new direction. Find a new stretch in the direction your body is now moving. Feel your muscles reaching out into the space. Good. Keep going until you can't go any farther and then curve again and find a new stretch in your new direction. Reaching out with your hands and fingers, through your shoulders, your chest, your ribs and your hips. Feel your whole body reaching and stretching. Feel yourself getting more room inside your body. Feel yourself reaching out, feeling taller, longer. Good. Keep reaching a little further. Reach through your whole body. Good.

Exercise 2: Reach Out—Partner

Mental Focus: I am sharing my energy with you.

Suggested Music: Same as Exercise 1

Position: Facing your partner arms-length apart. Elbows slightly bent.

Method:

1. Clasp hands around each other's wrists. Hold on tight.

2. Begin to bend your knees and pull back away from your partner. Only pull as hard as your partner is pulling so that neither one falls over. Begin reaching

back through your hips and let your head and back flatten out.

3. Keep pulling back away from your partner. Feel your shoulders and back stretch.

Exercise 2: Dialogue (Script)

Now, we're going to stretch with a partner. Say hello to your partner. Now stand facing your partner, arms-length apart. Clasp your hands together around the wrists and hold on tight. Slowly bend your knees and reach back through your hips. Be careful not to pull too hard. You don't want to pull your partner over. Feel for the balance point between you. Keep reaching back through your hips, letting your back flatten out. Feel the stretch through your back and shoulders. Adjust your feet if you need so you can get a good stretch and feel the balance point between you and your partner. Good. Keep reaching out through the hips. Enjoy the feeling of lengthening inside your body. Good. Slowly let yourself come back up. Keep the balance between you and your partner so that you are both stable when you come up. Good.

Power Up

Power Up is felt by engaging the muscles of the body and moving incrementally throughout the muscular system. As you engage one set of muscles, or one part of a muscle you release the others. The focus needs to be very specific, and a gradual shift of concentration between one point and the next is required. The slower you move, the deeper the contraction can be and the more energy is utilized.

The muscular system embodies our ability to act, to do and to manifest physically. Being able to move energy through the muscles enables you to connect the energetic system of the body with the muscular system. The muscular system is based on resistance. Being able to embrace resistance internally enables us to interact with our own systems and increase our power and ability to handle conflict. The muscular systems also help define the structure of the body, along with the skeleton. Thus learning to engage our own structure enables us to build and create structures that support us.

Purpose: This exercise develops inner and outer strength through fluid isometrics.

Exercise 1: Power Up—Individual

Mental Focus: I am strong and powerful.

Suggested Music: *One A.D.* by Various Artists, *Lie to Me* by Jonny Lang

Position: Standing, feet flat on the floor.

Method:

1. Clench your fists as hard as you can.

2. Let the rest of your body begin to tighten.

3. Move your body, but keep squeezing your muscles as tight as you can.

4. Keep going until you feel like you are going to burst, then let yourself shake and relax.

Exercise 1: Dialogue (Script)

Stand with your feet flat on the floor. Begin to squeeze your fingers towards the palm of your hand. Feel the muscles in your fingers and hands while you squeeze as hard as you can. Good. Keep squeezing. Let your wrists begin to move while you keep squeezing your hands. Feel the muscles in your arms begin to tighten. Squeeze them, too. Let your elbows bend and move, but keep squeezing your arm muscles. Feel how strong you are!

Now, squeeze through the shoulders, feeling the muscles in your shoulders. Keep squeezing. Squeezing through your back, too. Good. Keep squeezing. Squeeze through your chest and stomach, too. Feel your muscles. Feel how strong your muscles are. Good.

Now, add your legs. Squeeze your leg muscles. Feel how strong your legs are. Now squeeze through your whole body. Squeeze all your muscles. Keep squeezing. Let your body move very slowly, squeezing all your muscles as tightly as you can. Good. Keep squeezing. Keep squeezing. Keep going. Good.

Now let it go. Let your muscles soften and relax. Shake your body out. Reach out and stretch. Good.

Exercise 2: Power Up—Partner

Mental Focus: I am strong and you are, too.

Suggested Music: Same as Exercise 1

Position: Facing your partner.

Method:

1. Clasp hands together.

2. Push against each other allowing your shoulders, elbows and wrists to move very slowly. Only push as hard as your partner is pushing so that neither one falls over.

3. Use your entire body to push against your partner.

Exercise 2: Dialogue (Script)

Now, say hello to your partner. Face your partner. Keep your feet flat on the floor and bring your hands up to shoulder level. Clasp hands. Now, begin to push against your partner, but not so hard as to knock them over. Push against each other and let your shoulders, elbows and wrists move slowly while pushing against your partner. Feel your muscles working. Feel how strong your muscles are. Feel how strong your partner's muscles are. Feel how strong you both are. Good. Keep going. Pushing into each other's hands and moving very slowly. Feel your muscles. Good. Come back to starting position. Slowly, let your hands come apart and down.

Gotta Move

Gotta Move is felt by activating the vital energy of the body and moving incrementally at a quick tempo. Rapid movement that is fluid and specific allows for the opening and rejuvenation throughout the body.

By bringing your awareness to one area or moving between two points, either through repetitive or random movement, you revitalize an area that has capacity for more energy.

This form of movement is based in the bones, the skeletal system of the body. The bones, though porous, are the hardest areas within the body and create the foundation for our physical structure. Moving through the bones, around the bones and with the bones heightens our awareness of our skeleton and structure. It also frees up rigidity and tension that locks the bones in place.

Purpose: This exercise activates and moves vital energy through the entire body.

Exercise 1: Gotta Move—Individual

Mental Focus: I feel my energy and let it move.

Suggested Music: *Planet Drum* by Mickey Hart, *The Primitive Truth* by Brent Lewis

Position: Feet flat on the floor, as if they were stuck to it.

Method:

1. Move quickly in any direction through the knees, bending and straightening the legs.

2. Move quickly in any direction through the hips. Let the legs keep moving, too.

3. Move quickly in any direction through your ribcage. Let the legs and hips move, too.

4. Move quickly in any direction through your chest. Let the legs, hips and ribcage move, too.

5. Move quickly in any direction through your shoulders. Let the legs, hips, ribcage and chest move, too.

6. Move quickly in any direction through your elbows. Let the legs, hips, ribcage, chest and shoulders move, too.

7. Move quickly in any direction through your hands. Let the legs, hips, ribcage, chest, shoulders and elbows move, too.

8. Move quickly in any direction through your whole body.

9. Find new ways to move your body.

Exercise 1: Dialogue (Script)

Okay. We're going to get moving now. So, be sure you have plenty of room to move and make sure you won't hit anything. Okay. Stand with your feet flat on the floor. Now, let your attention move into your body. Notice any sensations occurring inside your body right now. Let your attention move down into your knees. Let your knees begin to move quickly. Allow them to move in any way they want to move. Good. Now, let your knees explore. Let them find new ways to move. Good. Keep going. Find a new way a move your knees. Let your knees move quickly. Good.

Now, focus on your hips. Let your hips move very quickly in any direction. Feel how your hips are moving. Let your legs and knees move with your hips, but keep your attention in your hips. Let your hips explore. Let them find a new way to move. Good. That's it. Let your hips have a life. Find a new way to move those hips. Good. Keep going.

Now, move up into the ribcage. Really let your ribs move. Feel your bones moving inside. Good. Find a new way to move the ribs. That's it. Have fun with your ribs. Good. Keep going, finding a new way to move the ribcage. Good.

Now, move up into the chest and shoulders. Let your chest and shoulders move very quickly. Feel the rest of your body moving with the chest and shoulders. Find a new way to move. Good. Really let the chest and shoulders move. Find a new way to move. Good. Keep going. Keep moving. Let your chest and shoulders move in a way they haven't moved yet. Good. Keep moving. Find a new way. Good.

Now, let your neck and head move with your chest and shoulders. Let them move very quickly. Good. Keep moving. Add your arms and hands and fingers. Let your whole body move quickly. Good. Keep going. Find a new way to move your whole body. Good. That's it! Let your body have fun! Good. Keep moving. Good.

Now slowly bring yourself back to starting position. Just stand for a minute and feel the energy inside your body. Feel the energy moving through your body. Good.

Exercise 2: Gotta Move—Partner

Mental Focus: I am feeling my energy with you.

Suggested Music: Same as Exercise 1

Position: Face your partner.

Method:

1. Let your hands touch, but do not hold onto each other.

2. Let your hands move very quickly while keeping in contact with your partner's hands.

Exercise 2: Dialogue (Script)

Now, say hello to your partner. Stand facing each other with your feet flat on the floor. Bring your hands up to shoulder height and let your hands touch. Let your hands begin to move very quickly while keeping in contact with your partner. Let your elbows and shoulders move with your hands. Notice how your hands are moving. Notice how your partner's hands are moving. Notice how your hands are moving together. Find new ways to move your hands with your partner. Keep your hands touching while you move. Good. Keep going. Moving very quickly. That's it. Find a new way to move with your hands. Feel how your hands are moving together. Good. Very quickly. Good. Slowly come back to starting position. Keep your hands together and feel the energy in your hands. Feel the energy in your partner's hands. Feel the energy between your hands. Good.

Dance Alive!

Dance Alive! is felt by focusing awareness, experiencing energy, expressing a sensation, in any form, position or tempo. It is the integration and combination of all the previous four types of movement put together. Being able to fluctuate between various systems, movements, positions, directions, tempos, rhythms, breath and sound demands that we become integrated and adaptable.

Dance Alive! is based in the energetic system, which is the electrical charge within each cell of the body. It is also known as the ethers or the space in between all physical manifestations in the body. When traveling through the energetic system, or open space, we can move through all systems of the body: fluid, connective tissue, muscular, skeletal and energetic as we move back and forth between them. This flexibility of focus allows us to experience how these systems work together and interact with each other. This is the foundation for our internal relationship within ourselves, being able to connect all systems and points of reference internally.

Purpose: This exercise allows one to practice all types of movement at the same time.

Exercise 1: Dance Alive!—Individual

Mental Focus: I express myself through my body.

Suggested Music: *Ray of Light* by Madonna, *Lost at Last* by Lost At Last

Position: Standing, feet flat on the floor.

Method:

1. The group leader calls out which movement to do (see script), and the children follow.

Exercise 1: Dialogue (Script)

Now, we're going to dance Follow the Leader. Find a place in the room and be sure you have enough room to move without hitting anything. Good. Stand with your feet flat on the floor and bring your attention to my voice. Ready. Here we go. Begin moving very quickly in any direction through your whole body. Good. Very quickly. Faster.

That's it. Keep going. Moving your whole body quickly. Now, squeeze every muscle you can. Every muscle you can. Squeeze. Tighter. Good. Keep squeezing. Find new muscles to squeeze. Let your body move and find new muscles to squeeze. Good. Keep squeezing.

Now, reach out. Reach out through your arms and fingers. Reach out through your shoulders and chest. Let your neck and head reach out, too. That's it. Really reach out into the room. Reach. Good. Now, let your arms and shoulders soften. Move very softly now right through the middle of your chest. Yes. Very slowly, very softly. Right through the middle of your chest. Feel your arms and shoulders and chest soften and relax. Good. Now, let your whole body move very softly, following the chest. Let your body soften and relax. Good. Keep going, softly, slowly. Now begin to reach out through the chest. Yes, reaching through the chest and now the ribcage. Reach out through the ribcage. Good.

Now the whole body. Reach out into the room with your entire body. Reach in any direction. Feel your body getting longer. Reach. Good.

Now, just shake it out. Let yourself move freely now. Moving in any direction, at any speed. Feel your body moving freely. That's it. Let yourself go. Enjoy moving freely. Good. Now, come back to starting position.

Exercise 2: Dance Alive—Partner

Mental Focus: I express myself with you, and you express yourself with me.

Suggested Music: Same as Exercise 1

Position: Facing your partner.

Method:

1. Dance with your partner, without touching.

2. Let your body move in any way that feels good to you while dancing with your partner.

Exercise 2: Dialogue (Script)

Now, say hello to your partner. Good. Stand facing your partner. Begin to dance in any way that feels good to you. Allow yourself to see your partner and see how your partner is dancing. Enjoy how your partner is moving. Enjoy how you feel dancing with your partner. Keep dancing and enjoy each other while you dance. Good. Bring your hands to shoulder level and let your hands touch. Begin moving your hands in any way that feels good. Notice how your hands feel moving. Notice how your partner's hands feel. Notice how your hands feel moving together. Good. Now, say thank you to your partner and move along again.

SECTION IV

Slim & Fit Forever

Fifteen

Talking to Your Child About Food and Fat

Interacting with your overweight child is a toughie. As my own mother used to say, "You're damned if you do, and damned if you don't! If I ask her about how her diet is going, she gets mad. If I ignore the fact that's she dieting, she thinks I don't care."

As I talk to parents around the country about coping with their children's fat, I realize that they are still as confused today as my own mother. Listen to what Yvonne Woods of Santa Monica, one of the original "guinea pigs" for the original *Beverly Hills Diet,* says about her dilemma in dealing with her own child's weight problem.

"Ezra was not only heavier than the other kids, he was also about two heads taller. When he'd tell me the kids called him names, it just broke my heart. Nothing I'd experienced in being a parent had prepared me to deal with this. I didn't know what to do."

What Yvonne and her husband Wayne emphatically didn't want to do was subject their growing son to a variety of diets. "I told him he was fine; he was beautiful," says Yvonne. "I told him he'd probably grow out of it when he hit puberty."

But puberty proved not to be the magic bullet for which his parents had hoped. By the time he was fifteen, Ezra was six-feet, one-inch tall and 235 pounds. His doctor recommended he lose at least thirty pounds. Even then he'd be at the top of the weight chart for his height and age. And what of all the hurt he had suffered in elementary and junior high school while waiting for nature to takes its course?

Then there's Lily Brumwell of Salt Lake City, Utah. Concerned about her daughter Sydnei who at age two was already the size of a five-year-old, she asked her pediatrician for advice. "Don't expect her to be small; her father's six-feet, eight-inches tall," she was told. "It's genetic. Don't talk about it because you'll just make her self-conscious." Yet by the time she got her physical for elementary school, under the section reserved for health concerns, her new doctor wrote "could become obese."

So how should you handle it when the kids taunt your child about being fat? Should you tell your child to ignore them because they're perfect or should you agree? How do you help them face the truth in order to become slim and fit? Of course you're at a loss for words. Up until now you haven't had a program that works or one that you could work with. But now there's *Slim & Fit Kids*.

In the following pages, you'll hear advice from two outstanding marriage and family therapists, Carol Yellin, M.F.T., who practices in Brentwood, California, and Ellen Jones, M.F.T., who does her in-person as well as long-distance telephone counseling from her West Los Angeles office. Do I agree with what they say? Yes and no. If your child is that special person who is sensitive and creative (an "eater"), things like teaching portion control and behavior modification don't work. We are dealing with innate characteristics. We first learn to assert ourselves, say yes or no, from birth with food. We say yes by sucking the breast or no by turning our mouths away. So it isn't all cut and dried, and physiologist don't necessarily have all the answers. *Sometimes mother knows best. . . .*

The question I'm most often asked by women with teenagers who are starting to get chubby around the middle—"not exactly fat," but on their way—is how to talk to them without hurting their feelings or throwing them into an eating disorder. So I've talked to two vital, slender women who have helped their own teenage daughters develop beautiful, healthy and fit bodies and minds, and included their real-life experiences. Both, you will learn, had very special reasons for treading gently.

Barbara Bassill is a svelte, gorgeous, high-level executive who is very disciplined and puts considerable energy into staying slim. Because she had a brief bout of anorexia during her own teen years, she's very sensitive about the way she talks to her own daughter, Natasha.

"I taught Natasha about nutrition when she was young," says Barbara. "When she recently asked me how she looked, I give her an honest answer. I told her she looked

Barbara and Natasha Bassill

great, which she did, but because I thought she could look better I asked her what made her ask me this question. She answered that she felt her tummy was getting fat. I asked her what in her daily food plan would create this. I wanted *her* to think and I wanted *her* to come up with the answer.

"She told me about her 'Cheerios and milk' snacks late in the evenings and several times during the day. I suggested to her to draw a picture in her mind of how she wanted to look and how this 'picture' would make her *feel*. She started working on her picture of herself, and she told me later how exhilarated she felt when she visualized this picture or image. She has added an exercise program that includes seventy-five to one-hundred sit-ups a day. She replaced Cheerios and milk with fresh-cut pineapple in the evenings and has a nice hot tea with honey. Not exactly Slim & Fit rules, but it works for her. But, then again, this whole 'exercise' worked for her. She was so exhilarated and high as a result of this newfound confidence that she has actively begun pursuing her dream of being an actress and has even gotten an agent."

Janice Vander Pol, a Beverly Hills Diet enthusiast with the cutest figure around, is the mother of three daughters and a son ranging in ages from four to twenty. Having endured and overcome bulimia herself, she didn't want the same thing to

happen to her teen-
age daughters in
their "obsession" to
be thin. All three of
them have become
advocates of *Slim
& Fit Kids*.

Janice kept her
interest in her chil-
dren's weight some-
what at a distance.

**Janice Vander Pol and her daughters,
Alia, Vanessa, Nicole**

"If I had tried to shove it down their throats,
or even suggest it for that matter, they'd dismiss it because it
was my idea. So I thought that if they watched me eat (I
love chips and salsa and big portions), they would be
encouraged. Well, I guess I was a good example because
they finally came to me (it took two years), and said, 'Mom,
how do we do it?' Now they're hooked. . . . and thin."

These women have found ways to help their children
grow up fit and slim. Listen now to what Carol Yellin and
Ellen Jones have to say and you'll have all the ammunition
you need to help your kids realize their dreams—being slim
and fit!

Don't Let Fat Sabotage the Family Dynamic

Carol Yellin, *a marriage and family therapist who has been working in Brentwood, California, for over twenty years treating kids at risk, has seen firsthand how kids suffer when they're obese.*

Carol Yellin

No one wants a child to be fat. But helping a youngster deal with weight that's out of control, rejection and/or ridicule by peers, a plummeting self-image and escalating health problems is a tough order. Overwhelmed by such concerns, parents too often shift the entire emphasis of the family onto controlling what the child eats and how much he or she weighs.

This is actually the biggest mistake parents make. Everyone in the family has his or her own issues to deal with. A sister may be having problems with geometry; a brother may be worried he won't make the basketball team. Mom may be concerned she won't get a much-needed raise. Dad may be struggling with balancing a job and going back to college at night. All of these concerns deserve just as much attention as a child's battle to control obesity.

How do you make sure everyone's included in the loop without placing undue emphasis on the child who seems most needy because he or she is fat? By shifting the emphasis away from losing weight to being healthy, and by including the child in attaining that goal.

It isn't good for you, the overweight child or the siblings for you to micromanage every morsel of food your overeater puts in her mouth. The message you really want to give your children is that your goal is to help him or her be fit and healthy, and food is one means to accomplish that. Rather than rule out some foods because they're fattening and force-feed others, get your child involved with the *Slim & Fit* program. This puts the child in charge of what he or she eats and the goal of becoming healthy.

It also gets you off the hook of being the food cop. Instead of saying, "Oh, no, don't eat ice cream; it's so fattening!" discuss how much ice cream the child really craves. This teaches kids to tune into their body's need for food rather than to just eat unconsciously. At the same time, they're learning when enough is enough and too much is too much.

Seeing your child come home from school crying because the other kids teased him about being fat or left her out of the games at recess can break your heart. What do you say to a five-year-old who's been called *Holly the Hippo* because she's so much bigger than all the other kids? Denying how she really looks can lead you into a disastrous trap—lying to your child. Of course we'd all like to be the white knight capable of slaying all our children's dragons, but telling a youngster he isn't fat when he is and promising to make the teasing stop by complaining to the parents of the teasers are at best temporary solutions. At worst, they prevent the child from developing problem-solving skills.

You can turn a very sad situation like this into a positive program for change by introducing your child to *Slim & Fit*. This extraordinarily extensive program will revolutionize the way in which overweight children eat by teaching them how to combine food, exposing them to self-esteem building exercises and introducing them to nontraditional fitness programs like "Work It Out with Thea!" and "Dance Alive!," which make it great fun to become active and lose weight.

At the same time, this program helps parents develop a dialog with their children to help them get in touch with their own feelings about their body image and learn some verbal self-defense skills. Acknowledge that the teasing must have really hurt his or her feelings. Brainstorm together ways your child might respond to the kids when it happens again. Share an experience from your own childhood about how you handled yourself when you were teased. This makes a child understand that teasing and being different are all part of the human experience, and part of growing up. Knowing that your child isn't alone and that such experiences are universal can actually lessen the hurt.

Then help your child get in touch with his or her own feelings about body image. Does your child think he or she is fat? If your child does, ask if he or she would like your help in becoming fit and healthy. Here's the perfect opportunity to introduce the eating philosophy behind *Slim & Fit Kids* that made *The Beverly Hills Diet* and *The New Beverly Hills Diet* so successful in helping adults overcome over-eating and gaining fat. Instead of making it your job to slim your child down, tackle it together by partnering with your child. You can turn overeating—often an excuse for rebellion—into a positive experience for both of you.

Pitfalls to Avoid in Helping Your Kid Get Slim & Fit

Ellen Jones *is a marriage and family therapist practicing in West Los Angeles with kids who have eating problems.*

Ellen Jones

Over the years I've discovered that if a child is going to lose weight and keep it off, both the child and the family must come to grips with a variety of complex social and psychological issues that affect the overeater, siblings, parents and the entire family unit.

Here are some pitfalls you'll want to avoid if you're trying to help your youngster get slim and fit:

1. *Wanting your child to look good so you look good.* Be sure your interest in your child's weight isn't a projection of your own compulsion to have a "perfect" kid. If your child's weight makes you anxious about how others view your parenting skills, discuss these feelings with a professional. Your goal is to keep your own feelings about yourself from making it more difficult for

your youngster to take responsibility for dealing with his weight.

2. *Being afraid to acknowledge accurately what the child already sees in the mirror or on the scales.* If your child asks for your opinion about his or her own body image, put the focus back on the child, asking the child to describe his or her own feelings about the way his or her body looks. If it's accurate, then you can agree. If not, express your own opinion honestly, kindly and nonjudgmentally.

3. *Nagging your child about eating and being fat.* Criticism only raises stress and anxiety levels, making the problem worse. Let youngsters know they are loved, valued and respected, regardless of how they look.

4. *Initiating discussions of weight, fat and food.* Listen for cues from your child that he or she is motivated to change his or her eating habits or body size. Once kids open the discussion, follow their lead. See if they can describe what they'd like to look like and eat like. Then ask if they'd like to look at some ways to accomplish this goal and if they want your help. Here's your chance to introduce *Slim & Fit Kids*. But don't be too fast to step in with a quick solution. Your child's job in life is to become an individual able to function independently, and your job is to allow that to happen.

5. *Overlooking the possibility that your child may be eating to cope with the stress of suppressed thoughts, feelings or experiences.* Learn to be a good listener, and be available if your child decides to confide in you. If your

own life is in chaos or your marriage in turmoil, know that this is going to have an effect on your child and your child's eating, so perhaps this would also be a good time to work on you.

6. *Assuming that your child understands nutrition, what constitutes a healthy diet and how to take good care of his or her body through exercise.* You can help by introducing and facilitating the *Slim & Fit* program and by setting a good example in terms of what and how you eat.

7. *Making exercise a punishment for being fat.* Bike together, take walks, play hoops, toss a ball around. Encourage your child to join some noncompetitive physical activity like dance, yoga, swimming and other activities that your child enjoys. Shape up together by exploring the nontraditional movement programs described in *Slim & Fit Kids.*

Most important, let kids know they are valued. Help youngsters believe in their personal worth by cherishing them for who they are, rather than for their performance. Focus on their positive unique qualities. Communicate often your faith in your child's abilities and intentions. Listening empathetically with your heart lets children feel they are respected and important to you. Building your child's trust in their lovability and capability bolsters a healthy sense of self. The more your child is able to accept and appreciate himself or herself, the more your child will have the motivation to make positive personal changes.

The Weight Is Over!

There you have it! The knowledge to combine food consciously; the inspiration from hearing other kids' stories, the exercise, the dialog, the insights from therapists and other parents. You know the right moves, the right words, the right formula for helping your kids get Slim & Fit!

Go for it. Together you have the power, the self-esteem and the knowledge to change your lives! The weight to be slim and fit is over!

Notes

1. "Annual Summary of Vital Statistics—1998." To be published in *Pediatrics* (Journal) December 1999. Data released to news media July 1999. Department of Population and Family Health Sciences, Johns Hopkins School of Hygiene and Public Health, Baltimore, Maryland.

2. Nancy Shonfeld-Warden, M.D., and Craig H. Warden, Ph.D., "Pediatric Obesity: An Overview of Etiology and Treatment," *Pedaitric Clinics of North America* 44, 2 (April, 1997): 339–355.

3. W. H. Dietz, "Therapeutic Strategies in Childhood Obesity," *Hormone Research* 39, 3 (1993): 86–90.

4. S. Rossner, "Childhood Obesity and Adult Consequences," *Acta Pediatrica* 87 (1998): 1–5.

5. Barry Sears, Ph.D., Mary Goodbody, *Mastering the Zone: The Next Step in Achieving Superhealth and Permanent Fat Loss* (New York: Harper Collins, 1996).

6. Judy Mazel, *The New Beverly Hills Diet* (Deerfield Beach, Fla.: Health Communications, Inc., 1996).

7. William H. Dietz, M.D., Ph.D., and Lorraine Stern, M.D., eds., *The American Academy of Pediatrics Guide to Your Child's Nutrition* (New York: Villard, 1999).

8. Richard P. Troiano, Ph.D., R.D., Katherine M. Flegal, Ph.D., Robert J. Kuczmanski, Dr.PH, R.D., Stephen M. Campbell, M.H.S., Clifford L. Johnson, M.S.P.H., "Overweight Prevelance and Trends for Children and Adolescents," *Archives of Pediatric and Adolescent Medicine* 149 (October, 1995): 1085–1091.

Two additional editorials critiquing methods of quantitating childhood obesity:

William H. Dietz, M.D., Ph.D., "Use of the Body Mass Index (BMI) as a Measure of Overweight in Children and Adolescents," *The Journal of Pediatrics* 132 (1998): 191–193.

Evan Chaney, M.D., "Childhood Obesity: The Measurable and the Meaningful," *The Journal of Pediatrics* 132 (1998): 193–195.

9. Clayton L. Thomas, M.D., M.P.H., *Taber's Cyclopedic Medical Dictionary* (Philadelphia: F. A. Davis Company, 1973), o–1, 2.

10. Richard E. Belrrman, M.D., ed., *Nelson's Textbook of Pediatrics,* 14th ed. (Philadelphia: W.B. Saunders and Co., 1992), 169–172.

11. T. N. Robinson, "Defining Obesity in Children and Adolescents: Clinical Approaches," *Critical Review of Food Science and Nutrition* 33 (1993): 313–320.

12. Samuel S. Gidding, M.D., Rudolph L. Leibel, M.D., Stephen Daniels, M.D., M.P.H., Michael Rosenbaum, M.D., Linda Van Horn, R.D., Ph.D., Gerald R. Marx, M.D., "Understanding Obesity in Youth," *Circulation* 94 (1996): 3383–3387.

13. "New Growth Charts for Children," *Drug Therapy Bulletin* 33, 12 (1995): 94.

14. L. D. Voss, T. J. Wilkin, P. R. Betts, "Do We Need New Growth Charts?" *Lancet 2,* 8556 (August 22, 1987): 447–448.

15. H. J. Binns, Y. D. Senturia, S. LeBailly, M. Donovan, K. K. Christoffel, "Growth of Chicago-area Infants, 1985 Through 1987," *Archives of Pediatric and Adolescent Medicine* 150, 8 (1996): 842–849.

16. U. Chike-Obi, R. J. David, R. Coutinho, S. Y. Wu, "Birth Weight has Increased Over a Generation," *American Journal of Epidemiology* 144, 6 (Sept. 15, 1996): 563–569.

17. R. Johar, W. Rayburn, D. Weir, L. Eggert, "Birth Weights in Term Infants. A 50 Year Perspective," *Journal of Reproductive Medicine* 33, 10 (October, 1998): 813–816.

18. W. H. Dietz, Jr., "Prevention of Childhood Obesity," *Pediatric Clinics of North America* 33, 4 (August, 1986): 823–833.

19. William H. Dietz, M.D., Ph.D., and Lorraine Stern, M.D., eds., *The American Academy of Pediatrics Guide to Your Child's Nutrition* (New York: Villard, 1999).

20. C. L. Williams, M. Bollella, B. J. Carter, "Treatment of Childhood Obesity in Pediatric Practice," *Annals of the New York Academy of Sciences* 699 (October, 1993): 207–219.

21. From *www.THRIVEonline.com* Parenting section. March 30, 1999.

22. William J. Klish, Ph.D., "Molecular Genetics of Obesity: Observations of a Rapidly Expanding Field," *In-Touch* 15, 3 (1998).

23. Richard E. Belirman, M.D., ed., *Nelson's Textbook of Pediatrics,* 14th ed. (Philadelphia: W. B. Saunders and Co., 1992), 106.

24. William H. Dietz, M.D., Ph.D., and Lorraine Stem, M.D.,

eds., *The American Academy of Pediatrics Guide to Your Child's Nutrition* (New York: Villard, 1999), 57.

25. Andrew Weil, M.D., *Natural Health, Natural Medicine* (New York: Houghton Mifflin Company, 1995), 25–30.

26. Katja Shaye, "Crazy for Cabbage," *Good Housekeeping* (July, 1996).

27. Andrew Weil, M.D., *Natural Health, Natural Medicine* (New York: Houghton Mifflin Company, 1995), 36–37.

28. Richard E. Behnman, M.D., ed., *Nelson's Textbook of Pediatrics,* 14th ed., (Philadelphia: W. B. Saunders and Company, 1992), 169–172.

29. John Robbins, *Diet for a New America* (Tiburon, Calif.: H. J. Kramer, 1987), 193.

30. Andrew Weil, M.D., *Natural Health, Natural Medicine* (New York: Houghton Mifflin Company), 25–30.

31. U. S. Barzel, L. K. Massey, "Excess Dietary Protein Can Adversely Affect Bone," *Journal of Nutrition* 128, 6 (June, 1998) 1051–1053.

32. R. P. Haeney, "Nutrition and Risk for Osteoporosis," *Osteoporosis* (San Diego: Academic Press, 1996), 483–505.

33. J. C. Juskevich, C. G. Guyer, "Bovine Growth Hormone: Human Food Safety Evaluation," *Science* 249, 4971 (August 24, 1990): 875–884.

34. Susan Gilbert, "Fears Over Milk, Long Dismissed, Still Simmer," *New York Times* (January 19, 1999): Health and Fitness.

35. David Steinman, *Living Healthy in a Toxic World* (New York: Perigree, 1996), 84.

36. David Steinman, *Living Healthy in a Toxic World* (New York: Perigree, 1996), 27.

37. Chrisitine Gorman, "Children's Menu," *TIME* 153, 13 (April 5, 1999): 84.

38. William H. Dietz, M.D., Ph.D., and Lorraine Stem, M.D., eds., *Guide to Your Child's Nutrition* (New York: Villard, 1999), 60–61.

39. Richard E. Beluman, M.D., ed., *Nelson's Textbook of Pediatrics,* 14th ed. (Philadelphia: W. B. Saunders and Company), 106.

40. Corrine T. Netzer, *The Complete Book of Food Counts* (New York: Dell, 1997).

41. Clayton L. Thomas, M.D., M.P.H., *Taber's Cyclopedic Medical Dictionary* (Philadelphia: F. A. Davis Company, 1973), N–45.

42. Judy Mazel, *The New Beverly Hills Diet* (Deerfield Beach, Fla.: Health Communications, Inc., 1996), 43.

43. Richard E. Behrman, M.D., ed., *Nelson's Textbook of Pediatrics,* 14th ed. (Philadelphia: W. B. Saunders and Company, 1992), 114.

44. Robert C. Whitaker, M.D., M.P.H., Jeffrey A. Wright, M.D., Margaret S. Pepe, Ph.D., Kristy D. Seidel, M.S., William H. Dietz, M.D., Ph.D., "Predicting Obesity in Young Adulthood from Childhood and Parental Obesity." *The New England Journal of Medicine* 337, 13 (September 25, 1997): 869–73.

45. William J. Klish, M.D., "Childhood Obesity," *Pediatrics in Review* 19, 9 (September, 1998): 312–15.

46. William H. Dietz, M.D., Ph.D., and Thomas N. Robinson,

M.D., M.P.H., "Assessment and Treatment of Childhood Obesity," *Pediatrics in Review* 14, 9 (September, 1993): 337–44.

47. Philip Fireman, "Asthma," *Primary Pediatric Care* (New York: Mosby, 1997), 1190–95.

48. William J. Kish, M.D., "Childhood Obesity," *Pediatrics in Review* 19, 9 (September, 1998).

49, 50, 51, 52. William H. Dietz, M.D., Ph.D., and Thomas Robinson, M.D., M.P.H., "Assessment and Treatment of Childhood Obesity," *Pediatrics in Review* 14, 9 (September, 1993).

53. J. Cook, R. Grothe, "Obesity in Children and Adolescents," *IOWA Medical Journal* 86, 6 (July-August, 1996): 243–45.

54. J. K. Mills, G. D. Andrianopoulos, "The Relationship Between Childhood Onset Obesity and Psychopathology in Adulthood," *Journal of Psychology* 127, 5 (September, 1993): 547–51.

55. Jane Gross, "Doctors See More Teens Opt for Cosmetic Surgery," *The Tampa Tribune-Times* (Sunday, November 29, 1998): 1, 14.

56. William H. Dietz, M.D., Ph.D., and Lorraine Stern, M.D., eds., *The American Academy of Pediatrics Guide to Your Child's Nutrition* (New York: Villard, 1999), 57.

Index

Also from Judy Mazel

The New Beverly Hills Diet

The best way to stay slim and fit for adults

Code #4258 • Paperback $12.95

The #1 *New York Times* bestseller teaches you Conscious Combining: how and when to mix different food groups for optimum weight control.

Imagine a diet where you can indulge in your favorite foods and still lose weight easily, and most importantly, maintain your new shape forever. Judy Mazel will make your dreams a reality.

Keep the Whole Family Slim and Fit with

Recipes to Forever

With delicious, mouth watering recipes, such as:

Tarte Provencal

Risotto with Asparagus

Cold Seafood Salad

Sesame Coriander Shrimp

Oven-Roasted Eggplant Napoleon

THE *New* BEVERLY HILLS DIET **RECIPES TO FOREVER**

JUDY MAZEL
#1 *New York Times* Bestselling Author

Code #4754 • Paperback $9.95

Judy Mazel shows you that staying slim doesn't have to be boring or bland. Also included are hints for adapting any menu to the Beverly Hills diet program.

The Perfect Pocket Reference

The New Beverly Hills Diet
Little Skinny Companion

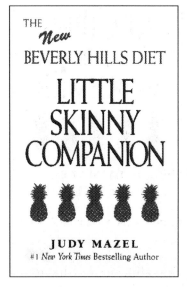

Code #4762 • Paperback $4.95

Essential information in this pocket guide includes:

- the Golden Rules of the program,
- the 35-day diet list,
- corrective counterparts to remedy miscombined meals,
- food group classifications,
- and a mini Born-Again Skinny Daily Diary for charting weight loss progress.

Indulge in the Audio!

The New Beverly Hills Diet Slim Kit

Four Audiocassettes and Diet Guide
(2 60-minute and 2 90-minute)
Code # 6501 • $24.95

Taking you beyond the reading experience, Judy herself joins you in this exciting audio set to get you on your way to a new, slim and fit you.

In each ten-minute session of Judy's daily audio program, she cajoles, motivates and instructs, arming you with the tools to build a lifelong maintenance philosophy.

Also included is *The New Beverly Hills Diet Little Skinny Companion.*

Slim & Fit Success Shop

Featuring a selection of
exciting products and services

- **THE SLIM & FIT SUCCESS KIT**
A Selection of snacks and cupboard-stockers to ensure your child Slim & Fit Success

- **SLIM & FIT SUPPLEMENTS**
Healthful additions to your new Slim & Fit Eating Program

- **SLIM & FIT INSURANCE**
Personal and private support is just a phone call or email away

- **CLUB SLIM & FIT**
Kids interacting with kids around the globe

- **CAMP SLIM & FIT**
Overnight program for kids and their folks

- **VIDEOCASSETTES**
Work It Out with Thea, Dance Alive!, Cooking with Christina and Francisco, Trigger-Point with Michael

- **AUDIOCASSETTES**
Work It Out with Thea, Dance Alive!, The New Beverly Hills Diet

- **THE NEW BEVERLY HILLS DIET BORN-AGAIN SKINNY TRILOGY**
The New Beverly Hills Diet, The New Beverly Hills Diet Little Skinny Companion, and *The New Beverly Hills Diet Recipes to Forever*

- **THE SPROUT JAR KIDS COLORING BOOK**
Pages of coloring fun, featuring the Sprout Jar Family

- **SPROUTS GALORE**
Jars and seeds to start your sprouting

- **SOUP TO NUTS**
A full-range "health-food store" featuring a plethora of non-perishable items available individually

For more information about these and other Slim & Fit Kids products and services or to place your order:

Call 800-510-7973
or Visit our Website at *www.slimandfitkids.com*